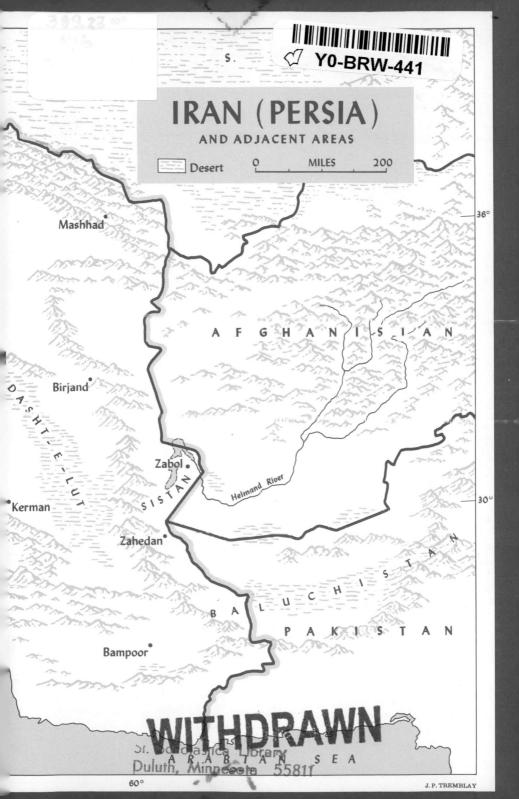

S.

IRAN (PERSIA)
AND ADJACENT AREAS

Desert   0   MILES   200

36°

Mashhad

A F G H A N I S T A N

DASHT-E-LUT

Birjand

Zabol

SISTAN

Helmand River

30°

Kerman

Zahedan

B A L U C H I S T A N

P A K I S T A N

Bampoor

WITHDRAWN

ARABIAN SEA

60°

J. P. TREMBLAY

A
WALL

·

AND

·

THREE
WILLOWS

·

Also by Najmeh Najafi and Helen Hinckley

Reveille for a Persian Village

Persia Is My Heart

A
WALL

AND

THREE
WILLOWS

Najmeh Najafi and Helen Hinckley

Illustrated with eight pages of photographs

Harper & Row, Publishers

New York, Evanston, and London

FIRST EDITION

LIBRARY OF CONGRESS CATALOG CARD NUMBER: 67-13690

C-R

To CARE
and the American people
who have given from their hearts
to help Sarbandan and to relieve
suffering everywhere

Contents

Photographs follow page 86

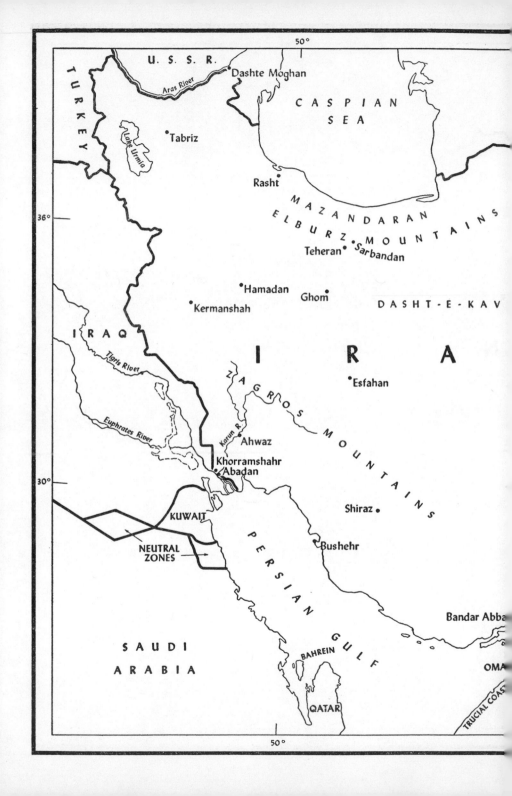

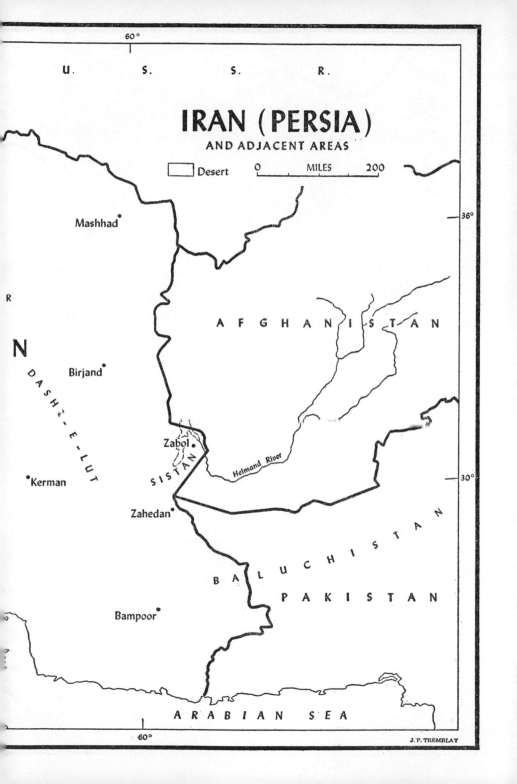

I ❧ Sarbandan, My Village

Winter grasped the mountains of Iran in his relentless hands. From them he squeezed all life and light. The fields, stretching away from the rutted twisting road we traveled, were dead and gray and the plants and shrubs colorless skeleton stalks, brittle and bent. Even the earth-brown villages we passed seemed to be asleep.

"In California there are roses," I told my brother Mohsen. "Roses and oranges, and—"

"And Shapoor." For a moment he took one hand from the steering wheel to put it over mine. "I too have known loneliness, Najmeh-jun."

"You always know what I am feeling," I told him gratefully.

It was Mohsen who had known that although I had only a week with my family in Teheran I would want to come for a few hours at least to my village, Sarbandan. I do not own Sarbandan; Sarbandan owns me. Mohsen had left his business at the bazaar to bring me to the village before sunset. Of course it was Mohsen who now sensed how much I missed Shapoor, my husband.

When I had first met Shapoor he was working for the government in Damavand. He substituted for another engineer assigned to drive me and some of my charges to a hospital in Teheran. I had heard a story about him which made him seem different from all of the other men in government service. One morning he had had to leave his quarters very early and a boy saw him leave, slipped into his room and stole everything of value. The thief wasn't clever so he was caught very soon. Shapoor visited the boy in jail and took him fruits and sweets. How many young men who have never felt depri-

1

vation can understand the needs of a boy who has known only poverty? As we drove toward Teheran we talked of the people and of the frustrations and degradation that come with poverty. We discovered that we felt the same about many things. After we were married we built a home together in Sarbandan and as we built it we dreamed greater dreams. Someday Shapoor should study in one of the Western nations. One cannot see his own country except in comparison and contrast with another. We might have planned to go to England, to Sweden, to Germany, but almost ten years before I had gone as a student to America; I felt that Pasadena was my second home and that we could quickly find a place for ourselves in that pleasant, familiar community.

Pregnant with my first child, I went with Shapoor to America. We settled into a tiny Pasadena apartment and soon Sina was born and my life began to follow the housewife's pattern. I had not known how difficult it is to do oneself the physical work that many servants do for us in Iran. I looked after my home, my baby, my loved guests. In America Persians are all one family, turning to each other as they would to kindred. Many times I was what my American friends called "bone tired," so I had decided to return to Iran before my second child was born. In Iran I would have his family and mine and I would be taken care of. Shapoor had completed less than three semesters of work so he would remain in college until he had completed his course, at least another year, perhaps longer.

The separation which I had thought would be tolerable when we made our plans in America now seemed to stretch far into the future. I was lonely. Lonely for Shapoor and for the friends I had left behind in America.

When Mohsen had suggested that we visit Sarbandan my sisters had objected to my traveling the winter-roughened road. "If this baby decides to be bounced out before her time, what will you do?" Fatemeh, my older sister, asked.

"There is a fine doctor in Sarbandan," I reminded her. "Many babies have been born in mountain villages. But I have come halfway around the world so what could less than a hundred kilometers mean to me now?"

"Carrying Sina with you," Fahkri, my other sister, said. "I don't know how you did it. At least you can leave him with us while you take this trip to Sarbandan. You don't need to fight him all the way."

I laughed. "He will sleep much of the time and he is only carsick when he is awake. Sina will be the pride of Sarbandan."

Even before Sina wakened we came abruptly to Sarbandan, folded in its gray hills. The village, beautiful in spring, in summer, in autumn, in the winter is dead and stark. Walls of sun-dried brick topped with rough thatch to protect them from the winter dampness are as brown and lifeless as the apricot and cherry branches lifting naked arms above them.

Perhaps it had been a mistake to come at this time. In the winter the men must leave the village and work in the rice fields of Mazandaran; many of the young women must seek work as servants in Teheran and send their wages home to their families to get them through the long, hard winters. As we drove past the shoemaker's little shop I looked out the window and called, "Yoo-hoo, anybody home?" The shoemaker is completely deaf but one of his children heard my call and looked out. "She has come back!" he shouted. "Lady Najafi has come back." Barefoot he ran up the narrow street calling at each door, "Lady Najafi is here. Lady Najafi."

Mohsen turned to the right toward my home—the home that Shapoor and I had built lovingly and with our own hands. Now the clinic doctor and his wife lived in the house but they would make us welcome.

The sound of our truck brought both the doctor and his wife to the door. "You are here," she cried, and we saluted each other with kisses. "We have been expecting you. We didn't know when, but we knew you'd come."

I looked at Mohsen and his eyes twinkled. "It was not difficult to send a message by Malek since each day he drives the bus."

"We have not told anyone else, though," the doctor said. "We knew you would want your visit to be a surprise."

The doctor's wife took Sina from my arms. "He's a fine boy," she said. "See how beautiful he is and so perfect."

"Shapoor is the proudest father in the world," I told them. "Always he says, 'My baby has such curly hair. My baby is so wide awake. My baby is smart; he learns everything quickly.'"

She laughed. "All men are alike." But I was reminded suddenly of the fact that she had no children—might never have—and I was ashamed that I had spoken of Shapoor's pride in our son. In California I had resented having a second child so soon, resented returning without my husband, resented my awkwardness, my inability to study in an advanced course as I had planned. Now I heard her say, "All men are alike," and I was ashamed, too, of my resentment.

Almost before I had washed my face and hands and put clean clothing on Sina, the people of the village were at the door. "We must have a party," I said. "Why didn't I bring food?"

"Why do you suppose I brought the truck instead of the small car?" Mohsen asked. In a moment he brought in a whole barbecued lamb as well as armloads of other food, all prepared for the eating.

"Mohsen!" I said, and the tears came suddenly to my eyes.

Someone evidently had advised the people to wait quietly until the party was ready, for we heard no more calling and stamping of feet from the front porch; but when we threw open the doors the villagers joyfully came in. There was Mash'hadi Mokhtar, the owner of the teahouse who had been the source of information to me all the time that I had worked in Sarbandan. With him were his brothers, Musi and Malek. These young men were not working in the rice fields of Mazandaran because Mash'hadi Mokhtar was the village capitalist and he had enterprises that kept his brothers busy. There was Mohradi, the tall Kadkhoda. In the Iranian village the kadkhoda is like a mayor except that he is usually not elected for a limited term of office. In the old days when villages were owned by great landlords the kadkhoda, chosen by the landlord, was his agent in the village and had the responsibility of being both the governor and the overseer. In many villages the kadkhoda was a hereditary position. In new Iran, since the land reforms have made many men landholders, the kadkhoda is selected by the people with the approval of the government. In Sarbandan there were two kadkhodas, each chosen by one of the two tribes that live in the village. The tall Kadkhoda was in charge of the settled people of the town, the short Kadkhoda of the shepherds who lived in town only part of the year. With Mohradi was his wife, Banu, and his sister Massemeh. After I had greeted them I asked, "And Madar-i-Kadkhoda [mother of the Kadkhoda], where is she?"

"Tonight she brings a baby. The young mother was in need."

An excellent clinic, an excellent doctor, and still the women were in need of the ancient midwife who offered wonderful magic potions and never washed her hands before bringing a baby. Madar-i-Kadkhoda was a woman long past eighty who had learned all the doubtful wisdom of an earlier age.

I turned to greet Kutchiki, the short Kadkhoda. "You are welcome here." He was especially welcome since he seldom came even to the Rish e safed, the council of village elders. "You must have some lamb, some tea, some sweets."

In spite of the chatter I could hear the boiling of the water in the *samovars*. There would soon be tea for everyone. In the next room, my bedroom when I, myself, lived in this home, Sina was being shown to the admiring villagers. He had finished with his carsickness and was laughing, waving his arms, and gleefully showing off every word, both English and Farsi, in his vocabulary.

"A beautiful son. A beautiful son," the villagers said, and I knew that now that I had borne a son I was a complete woman in their eyes.

In the kitchen Asghar, who had been my servant when I lived and worked in Sarbandan, was taking charge of the preparation and the serving of the food. Busily helping him was a slender boy of perhaps fourteen, with sparkling black eyes and hands as clean and well kept as a woman's. I didn't remember him so I pointed him out to Mash'hadi Mokhtar. "Who is that boy?" I asked. "Should I know him?"

"You should," he replied, "but at his age boys and girls change so rapidly. His name is Ramazan."

"Is his mother a widow?" I asked.

"A widow? No. Why?"

"After a time I will need servants. I plan to employ a houseboy and a woman to care for the children. A young man with a widowed mother would be exactly right."

Mash'hadi Mokhtar grinned. I noticed that he had come in such a hurry that he had neglected to slip over his own strong teeth the shining gold crowns that spoke of his position in village high finance. "Right now his father is working in Mazandaran; but to my latest knowledge he is not dead."

"Oh, well, Ramazan is not the only village boy but he looks clean and awake."

"His aunt is widowed. Would that serve you?"

"Perhaps." There was something about the boy that was especially appealing. To have him in my home as a servant would be to take something of Sarbandan with me.

I turned to greet another visitor, Eshrat, a stubborn woman who had been most unteachable. "You have a beautiful son. They say he is an American citizen. But he looks like any other Persian baby. How is this?"

"He looks like his father, many say," I told her.

"But still he is American," she insisted.

"And Persian," I smiled, turning to the next guest who waited to talk to me.

Many wanted to talk of the clinic. The doctor was excellent. His wife was good and thoughtful and wise. All was neat and clean and shining. In all of the villages there was not such another clinic.

Others wanted to talk of the bath. So pleasant it is to go to a clean bath with one's children about one. Each naked child can be scrubbed clean as a bone while the mother sits and talks with her neighbor in the pleasant steam. At first the villagers had preferred a pool to a series of shower heads, but now that they were used to running water they were happy. The bath was so inexpensive that everyone could be clean. The hammami, the bathkeeper, was so efficient that there was always hot water.

Others wanted to talk of the school. The boys' school should grow. They had hoped this winter for a seventh grade but still the sixth grade was the top class. Not everyone was in school, of course. Perhaps half—perhaps even more. There is the problem of shoes, they reminded me. If a mother has four sons and one pair of shoes she must decide as soon as winter comes which son should wear the shoes and go to school. If there were only more shoes—more money to buy shoes.

There was so much still to be done in Sarbandan, I thought. Perhaps after the new baby was born and I was strong again . . . Perhaps . . .

A shy young woman broke into my thoughts. "Lady Najafi, you do not remember me. I am Batool."

"You are Batool? But you are walking!" During my first year in Sarbandan I had sent this same girl to a hospital in Teheran and there they had amputated her leg below the knee to save her life.

"I am walking. I even dance. Lady Najafi, I don't have words to tell this, but each new morning I wake up to this beautiful world and say, 'I am alive!' If you had not been in Sarbandan I wouldn't be living now."

"But you are walking!"

"My artificial leg works very well. It was a gift from one of your friends who doesn't want his name known." For only a moment she was silent. "Lady Najafi, I am to be married when the men return from Mazandaran. Mahmoud, my cousin, knows of this artificial leg. He doesn't mind. And I am happy."

There were other women—all those who had been in my sewing and sanitation classes, each eager to tell me of a new child, a new accomplishment, some advancement in a way of life. I listened to each, and finally I sat down on the floor and let people sit beside me. It was now late November and my baby would be born in early January. I wearied too easily. And yet, "Where are the boys and girls?" I asked Hagaar, the wife of the shoemaker.

"They are at home. Surely there is no room for children tonight."

But I heard in my memory the glad voice of her young son as he raced barefoot over the frozen ground calling, "She's here. Lady Najafi has come again."

"The lamb may be gone," I told her, "but there are always sweets and tea."

I didn't see a messenger leave my home but soon the children came like the swift-flowing jube in spring, spilling through the house. Sarbandan had never seen such a party, not even for a wedding.

"Little Rabbit," I said, seizing one six-year-old by the foot as he passed by. "Did someone serve you?" The boy with the bullet-round head, the close-cropped black hair and the wild ruddy color in his cheeks stopped to look down upon me. "I am no longer little Rabbit," he said. But he held a large piece of bread in one hand, two cookies in the other. He had ever been a great eater.

At last the food was gone, the humming samovar was quiet and most of the guests had left, with the request, "Please don't stay away so long, Lady Najafi."

Before he left, Mohradi, the Kadkhoda, sat for a moment beside me. "We should have a meeting of the Rish e safed," he said. "There are many problems and we need your wisdom."

"There are always many problems," I answered, feeling their weight settle on my shoulders, "but you see I have problems of my own. Today I came to Sarbandan not to give strength but to gain it."

"Some other time? Soon?" he asked.

"Some other time," I answered.

For I had plans for Sarbandan, plans to really bring the village into the twentieth century, but these must wait, at least for a time.

When the guests had gone, Mohsen, the doctor and his wife and I sat together on the floor. Asghar and the young boy Ramazan had tidied up the kitchen and put the trays, the jugs, the jars back into the truck.

Almost in his clinical manner the young doctor asked, "Will you have this baby in Teheran?"

"Both Fahkri and Fatemeh have invited me to their homes and my mother would care for me. But no, I shall not bear this child in Teheran."

The young doctor's face was alight. "Perhaps in Sarbandan then. We could give the best of care to you and the boy would be our joy to watch over while you regained your strength."

"You are so kind." Tears came to my eyes—perhaps of weariness, perhaps of gratitude to these dear people, perhaps of both.

"I am going south to Ahwaz to bear this child."

"Ahwaz!" They spoke the name together as if I had mentioned Samarkand.

"At present Ahwaz is the home of Shapoor's parents. Since he is still in America it is suitable for me to go to his mother for the birth of her grandchild."

"I see," the doctor said. "I can understand what your husband must feel being separated from you at this time."

"I too am hurt by this separation," I wanted to say, but my lips were closed. I had just realized that all through this gay, loving evening I had not missed Shapoor.

2 ❦ No Ruz in Teheran

NO RUZ IN IRAN. IN PASADENA SHAPOOR WOULD BE ATTENDING classes as usual, perhaps noting that it was March 21, 1959, perhaps remembering that I had been gone for five months. But in Iran it was the New Day, the New Year. Everywhere in Teheran there are gift giving, gaiety, laughter, much visiting from place to place. The spirits of the people, after a long, cold winter, rise like sap in the greening trees; rise and overflow and encompass friends and kindred—even strangers. For in my country the first day of spring is the first day of the New Year, and for all Iranians the first day of a new and better life. In the midst of all the celebrating I sat in my mother's house trying hard to keep my sadness from diluting the happiness of the rest of the family.

"You are unhappy, Najmeh. Why?" Mohsen asked, turning me gently so that the light from the window fell across my face.

"Yes, I am unhappy," I agreed, "but why?" I turned my face away from him so that he would not see the tears dampening my lashes. "Who knows?"

My mother bringing me tea and an arrangement of flowers guests had brought to welcome me home had heard Mohsen's question. "Najmeh is tired. The journey from America. The birth of Nassim. Her illness since she came to us here."

"Perhaps," I answered. Yes, I was tired but there was something more. I was weighted with anxiety. Shapoor and I are not wealthy and one does not go to school in America at no cost. I had thought as soon as the baby was born I would find work to do in Teheran to support myself and the children. Instead I had returned from the

10

South to the extreme cold of Teheran and had developed pneumonia. Now my assets were almost gone. Any of my brothers and sisters would willingly have assisted me, but I had been independent for a long time and I could not go back to dependency. There was much to do in Sarbandan but before I could go on with that work I must solve the problem of my own financial situation.

I had other worries, too. I had gone to Ahwaz to have the baby as Shapoor had suggested and because I knew that this was something he really wanted. He wanted me to grow closer to his parents, his parents closer to me. Instead the time spent with them had had the opposite effect. They were terribly crowded in the only apartment that was available to them. In Ahwaz there is always a shortage of possible rentals and landlords prefer not to rent to anyone associated with the army or with the government. Shapoor's father was associated with both.

Although they were accustomed to a pleasant home, beautifully furnished, the best apartment they had been able to procure in Ahwaz was a cramped two-room apartment. They moved over to make room for me and I knew how inconvenienced they were. They gave me one of the rooms and in it I had to keep myself, Sina, the new baby and all of my things. I made Nassim's bed on a pile of suitcases to keep her out of Sina's curious reach. I tried, we all tried, but tensions developed nevertheless. About this I was concerned.

Now there was my health. Every plan of my life depended upon my being strong, healthy, able to stand any change, any hardship.

"I am tired," I said. "Tired and worried."

I had sat in my mother's house with my baby daughter in my arms, Sina standing at my side whining to take Nassim's place on my lap, or peeking out like an inquisitive squirrel when anyone came to call, and received visitors. I had showed my children off with a mother's pride, I had chatted gaily of life in America, I had listened to accounts of births, deaths, marriages, business successes, social successes which had occurred since my departure.

During No Ruz everyone must visit all his relatives and friends. The streets are crowded with the poor who walk. The buses are filled—some passengers even clinging to the outside—with the near-poor. The taxis, which in Teheran are inexpensive, carry those who have a few coins in their pockets, and those who have money ride in their own cars, some behind liveried drivers, some driving them- selves, honking joyfully through the crowded streets.

"I am tired," I admitted, ashamed of the tears that insisted on dropping off my cheek onto Nassim's soft shawl. "I . . . please, I can see no more guests."

Mother, Fahti and Mohsen left me. I began to sing an old song to the children—all about a rabbit who was both wise and good. In a moment Mother returned. "Najmeh, it is Dr. Birjandi. He has come asking for you."

Dr. Birjandi was a long-time friend of the family and it was not surprising for him to visit us on No Ruz. But for a moment I was surprised that he had asked for me. Perhaps my sister Fahkri had told him that I had returned from America and that I was eager to work for my people again. When I had returned from America after attending school in California I had insisted that I wanted to work directly with my people, and it was my sister who had sent for Dr. Birjandi, the director of all such work in Iran. He had come to dinner and after dinner we had sat alone on an island of our mutual interests, washed by a sea of conversation and laughter from the other guests. For more than two hours we had talked. He had told me of the work of the Development Bongha in rural areas. The Bongha has no counterpart in America. It is like a government bureau, except that it is far more independent. It is like a founda- tion, except that the funds come from the government and not from private sources. It is like an institute except that its research and educational facilities are in the field of operation. The Bongha, he told me, is the most forward-moving organization in Iran. He also told me of American Point Four, of the Ford Foundation, of the Near East Foundation. But, more important, he had listened to my plans to work for my people and had said gently, "I know you want to help your people, Najmeh; but you have too much heart. You will have to educate it to be strong, not soft. If you fail in this work it will be because you love—too much."

At his suggestion I had worked for a time for the Near East

Foundation. After I had left the Near East Foundation and had begun, with the help of a Ford Foundation grant, my own work in Sarbandan, Dr. Birjandi had watched my progress with special interest.

Now as Mother waited in the doorway for my reply I was glad that the family had such a friend, a man whom no one could accuse of dishonesty or corruption and who knew my own need to work for my people.

"Dr. Birjandi! Of course I will see him."

Mother took Nassim and led Sina, protesting, away to play with his cousins.

It was good to see Dr. Birjandi, perhaps a little grayer, heavier, balder than when I had left, but with the same quiet assurance in his voice, the same soft twinkle in his eyes. Even what might have been the same coat folded over his arm. This he gave to the houseboy who had served me since my return from Ahwaz, and took the seat across the low table from me.

"You are well?" he asked, studying me from under slightly lowered lids. I nodded and waited for him to finish the pleasantries that no Persian ever bypasses no matter how urgent the business. Then his face changed quickly, mirroring his thoughts as a Persian's face does when only perceptive friends are present.

"You have a grave problem?" I asked.

"Yes." And then he sighed. Abruptly he sat forward with his elbows on his knees. "Have you been to Baluchistan?"

"Baluchistan? No."

Ramazan brought the tea and I served it, my eyes still on Dr. Birjandi's face.

He drank the tea, then replaced his tea glass on the tray and pushed the tray aside. "I know every mile of Baluchistan." Then his face crinkled around his eyes in his special smile. "I couldn't hide that if I wished to, since my name Birjandi says that I come from Birjand on the Afghanistan frontier." He traced a map on the table before him. "Here is Afghanistan and south of Afghanistan is Pakistan. And here on the border is Sistan Baluchistan." The map was not on the table but in our minds. "And here is Bampoor—the poorest city in the world."

"The Baluchi are nomads?" I tried to gather in my memory all that I had heard of this place.

"Yes. Most of them. Sistan Baluchistan has an area of 100,000 square miles and only 500,000 people. Just five people for each square mile. There may be even fewer. An accurate count has never been made."

"But Bampoor is a city, you said."

"Yes, some kind of city. Perhaps 4,000 people including the nomads who go and come. There are 1,740 villages in all of Baluchistan, but only 200 people, or even fewer, live in each village. The villages come and go, too, since most of the people live in tents and follow the grass from the mountains to the plains and back to the mountains again. They are at home wherever they unfold those black tents."

"But they are satisfied with their lives?"

"Those who know no better are satisfied." He was silent for a moment, caressing the second glass of tea, which Ramazan had just brought him. "Once Baluchistan was the granary of Iran. Now it is nearly all desert. It can be productive again if we can find the lost underground water supplies, if we can construct irrigation canals, build river dikes and dams. Najmeh, there is so much to be done it defies the imagination."

"But the Development Bongha will do it?"

"We shall try, but we must move slowly, slowly. We may both be dead and buried before the ripening wheat waves over the plains of Sistan Baluchistan." Then he laughed at his own discouragement and in a changed voice began to talk of other things. "The government wants the nomads to settle in permanent villages. Settlement has been desirable for a long time. Now it is imperative." Then he talked of the prospecting for uranium and for oil, the possibility that neighboring nations would push over the sparsely settled border. He spoke of the Italconsult, an engineering consultation firm from Rome that had undertaken a coordinated development program in the region; of the agricultural program that had already been established, of its successes and failures. He did not need to speak of the lack of national spirit among tribesmen since we both knew the nature of nomads.

"The nomadic life is a harsh life for women." Dr. Birjandi leaned forward, holding to the edge of the table with both hands. "Najmeh, you can't imagine what life is like for women and children in a primitive society. I have been all over Baluchistan by camel. I have been on the plains and in the mountains. I have seen how the people live." He was silent for a minute then said abruptly, "Like animals. Exactly like animals."

He talked then of the power of the khan—in Baluchistan called the *sardar*—who can sell the people with the village if he wishes to; who owns the very dates on the trees so that the farmers can have only the dates that fall, or the pits from the dates pitted for shipping to Kuwait and Amman. "Like animals, exactly like animals," he repeated.

"Have you established a woman's program in Bampoor or in any of the villages?" I asked.

"We planned such a program for Bampoor and the six nearest villages. We thought that the work might spread to the three hundred villages now included in the Italconsult project. But—no woman director will go to Baluchistan."

"The heat perhaps."

"Sometimes 130 degrees, but of course during the hottest months we do not try to operate the program." I passed him the sweets but he motioned them away with the back of his hand and lit a cigarette instead. "It is the loneliness. It is the wall that these people have built between themselves and any change. The language is different, the traditions are different; but most important they stubbornly resist what we try to do for them. No one can reach the heart of the women."

"I'll go," I said abruptly. "Some of my girls will go with me."

"They need you, Najmeh. They don't know that they need you, but they do."

He rose and took my hand. His face was lighter and so was my heart.

Allah had been good to me. The work in Baluchistan would

relieve me of financial worries and would give me a chance to grow. I had always risen to the challenge of something really difficult, especially when accepting the challenge meant serving my people.

After Dr. Birjandi had left I heard Sina crying somewhere outside the house. Sina, who had been the only child in a houseful of adults in Pasadena, had not yet learned to get along with other children. He tried to get his way through force and if he tried this method with his larger cousins he frequently was hurt. I was on my way to comfort him when abruptly I stopped. Suddenly I knew that never again—not, at least, until Sina and Nassim were grown—would I have the right to say as I had just said to Dr. Birjandi, "I will go." The realization was like a physical blow. I sat down on the floor, my ears almost closed to my son's loud cries. For a time I had forgotten Nassim, accustomed to my arms, and Sina always dragging at my skirts. With my feet folded under me, my face between the knuckles of my two hands, I faced the reality. I was no longer Najmeh. I was a mother. Now and forever I would have to choose between trying to help the unfortunate people in my country and looking after my own babies.

My mother came in, leading Sina, who was still rubbing one little fist into his eyes. "There was no real trouble," she said. "Sina is not hurt. Only angry."

I looked up into my mother's clear blue eyes and she dropped down beside me. "What is it, Najmeh-jun?"

"Mother dear, Dr. Birjandi did not come for a friendly No Ruz call."

"I know that."

"He wants me to organize a woman's program in Baluchistan."

"You will go, Najmeh?"

"I said I would go." I felt compelled to tell her about the moment of truth that had just shaken me, but I knew that I had no words. No words that would bridge a generation.

My mother had been married when she was twelve. All of her adult life she had been a widow, rearing her family according to the Persian traditions. My mother wore a chadar in the old manner; her face was never uncovered when a strange man was present. Every day of my childhood I had seen her pray in the traditional way. How could this mother of Old Persia understand the quickening pulse of her country? And yet she did and said, "You must go, Najmeh-jun. I will care for the babies."

"Baluchistan is not far by plane. I will tell Dr. Birjandi that there must be a plane available to bring me often to my family." I got to my feet and went to find Nassim. My arms wanted her softness.

Now that I again felt useful, my feet, my hands, even my thoughts lost their weariness. Already the agricultural mission in Baluchistan was at work. I must move quickly with the woman's program. Always I had felt that any program should be introduced slowly—nothing should be given until the people, themselves, had recognized the need. In Sarbandan I had moved very slowly. I had taken with me from Teheran untrained girls who lived in my home as if they were my sisters. They had first found themselves, then learned to understand the village people and finally had helped to carry on the work of the village. In Baluchistan, since the program had already begun, perhaps the woman's program could be introduced more rapidly and I would need to start my work with trained personnel. Naturally I thought first of my own girls—those whom I had trained at Sarbandan: Farkandah, Effat and Pooran. To them I wrote:

"This is Najmeh. She wishes to work in Bampoor, Baluchistan. If you can still stand her, and if you still believe in her, come Friday morning." And I gave the address of my mother's home.

In Sarbandan I had once interviewed a trained dehyar (village worker), Pahvine. Pahvine was in her middle thirties and had a husband with an incurable disease and three teen-aged daughters who depended upon her for support. She had come from an excellent family and I remembered her as being a gentle, attractive woman with very dark skin, black curly hair and expressive dark eyes. We had talked about the classics and she had recited for me long excerpts from Hafiz. But more important to me was that she was expert at cooking, home management, and the handling of money. To her I wrote:

"This is Najmeh. She wishes to . . ."

After I had written the letters I set to work to learn all I could about Baluchistan. On the map I found that it was watered by the River Helmand and that it was near Hamoun Lake, and I read that Afghanistan, through which the River Helmand flows, was disputing with us about the use of the water. I read, too, more of the prospects for large uranium deposits in the area. Almost at once a seemingly valueless strip of land could change to one of highest value. I also found that in the area there were some five thousand immigrants from Afghanistan and Russia. Had these five thousand come looking for a better life or was this planned infiltration?

I spent the days in planning, the nights in dreaming of the project, and suddenly it was Friday and Pooran was at my mother's door asking for me. Pooran, who was so much like an angel. In her childhood she had had polio and now she stood scarcely to my elbow—and I am less then five three. The spine that should have held her head higher than mine was bent in a loop and created a hunched back. But her legs and arms were normal and her face was beautiful. Her skin was glowing and fair, her hair heavy and dark, her smile constantly showing teeth incredibly white. This Friday morning she wore a white skirt—new for No Ruz, I thought. Her dark jacket with a demure white round collar was full over the shoulders to cover the misshapen back. I smiled to see her pristine white gloves, her elegant high-heeled shoes. With her she had brought not only a large shining new handbag but a suitcase, a bedroll, and a roll of additional blankets. At Sarbandan we had always said that Pooran needed more blankets than anyone. In a neat cotton bag she carried the pillow that she needed to rest her back whether sitting or reclining.

I had not written to the girls to bring their suitcases as I had planned to spend this morning in discussion.

Soon Farkandah and Effat came, not together but a few minutes apart. They did not bring their suitcases or bedrolls. And after we had drunk tea together I learned why. Both Farkandah and Effat were already employed in villages where they felt they were giving valuable service. Pooran had applied for important work with the Development Bongha but she had been rejected because of her deformity.

When Pahvine came she, also, had her suitcase and was ready to leave for Baluchistan. Her husband was in a hospital; her daughters she could leave for a time with relatives. Later she would want to have them with her.

All morning the five of us, Farkandah, Effat, Pooran, Pahvine and I, drank tea and talked. Although Farkandah and Effat were not free to go with us they were as interested as if they, too, were starting on this new adventure. I did not know what we would be expected to accomplish in Baluchistan. The big aim, to make the life of the Baluchi woman better, was clear of course, but at this point we could not tell how this could best be done. Improvement in sanitation, training in child care? Who knew? Sometime we would try to do some of the things we had done in Sarbandan, I told Pooran, but my philosophy is to go slowly, slowly, letting people sense their own needs before we offer to fill these needs.

At noon Farkandah and Effat kissed Pooran and me good-bye. Pooran and Pahvine left their suitcases and bedrolls with me. I would let them know what day we would leave.

And before we were ready to leave for Baluchistan the Development Bongha sent me another assistant, Zahra, a young girl with a bridge of freckles across her pretty nose, dark hair swinging just below her elbows. She was dainty and pretty and untried, but she wanted to join us so I agreed.

3 ❧ The Border

WHEN I DECIDED TO GO TO BALUCHISTAN I BECAME A DIFFERENT woman—alert, alive, happy, confident. Now I could enjoy caring tenderly for my baby, Nassim, taking Sina on my lap to talk or sing to him. Sina seemed to know that I was planning to desert him and he clung to me, his sweet round face puckered sorrowfully and his great brown eyes tried to draw the truth from mine.

There were delays that gave me a few extra days with my babies. We had planned to leave directly after "thirteenth day out," the last day of the No Ruz celebration, but Dr. Birjandi had planned for fifty men to accompany us to Baluchistan—engineers, social workers, agricultural experts, medical advisors—and we must wait for these men, recruited from all over Iran, to gather in Teheran. Dr. Birjandi, in touch with all of the rural problems of Iran, still felt that Baluchistan was the most important field in which to do intensive work.

When the time came actually to leave the children I could scarcely stand to go. As a young girl I had left my mother, my brothers and sisters, when I went to America to study. I had wondered fleetingly if I would ever see them again but the excitement of going had precluded any sorrow. I had left a very real part of myself in America when I had returned to Iran without Shapoor. But leaving the children was different. I had never been away from Sina since the day of his birth and Nassim, barely three months old, seemed so infinitely fragile and precious. I knew that they would receive excellent physical care and that my mother would give them gentleness and love; but still, leaving them brought indescribable emotions. I comforted myself that the Baluchistan project could not operate in the heat of the summer and in a few months I would be home for a time. Dr. Birjandi had promised that a plane would be available to bring me home if any emergency arose; but as I unwound Sina's arms from around my neck and wiped his face, flushed and swollen from crying, these promised comforts seemed too, too distant.

The company of men, experts in many fields, my girls and I left Teheran in a motor caravan. Dr. Birjandi had preceded us by plane to set up the eight-day conference he planned to conduct before we began our work. My girls were riding in one station wagon; I in another.

Nowhere in Iran are the roads excellent though the beautifully engineered road that joins the Caspian Sea with Teheran is one of the most spectacular in the world. The road we would follow south toward Isfahan is dusty and filled with jolting holes and the road east toward the Afghanistan border is especially primitive. Camels may travel with comfort; perhaps mules and even horses. But cars, no. The loose sand pours between the wheels, the car slips, the dust rises in clouds that cut off all visibility, and the holes hidden under the powdery surface wait to break the axle of any car that drops into them. Slowly, slowly the caravan would inch along. Then, made bold by the seemingly safe passage, the drivers would burst into dangerous speed, sometimes skirting on two wheels the great rocks that frequently rest in the middle of the road. How white and all-engulfing is the desert as it stretches to the horizon on every side. There were miles without any villages, without any greening fields, without any evidence that we were crossing the land of the living.

At length we came to two date palms in a tiny oasis and we knew that a village was near. Again we came to a ragged cemetery, overgrown with dry weeds piled high against the irregular stones placed side by side; then we knew that we were within walking distance of another small oasis and mud village. We were uncomfortable, dirty, thirsty, and there were no refreshment stands nor restrooms.

On we went from oasis to oasis across the lifeless desert. At last we stopped for the night at Zahedan, the capital of Baluchistan and rails' end for the Iranian railroad. Here we visited the town's most famous sage. He was old, but bright-eyed and talkative, and he had an awesome mustache undulating over his broken, scraggled teeth. He told us that he had twelve wives, then he corrected himself to say that eight were concubines. In Iran the concubine has legal status. She goes through a ceremony which is much like a marriage ceremony except that it has a time limit and is self-dissolving. He called his wives, who looked shyly through an open doorway but did not enter. Four of them were pregnant—a fact that he was preposterously proud of.

One of the engineers asked lightly about the love that twelve women must be content with.

"Have you been to the zoo?" The polygamist twitched his great mustache. "Some birds need one love, others need many."

He laughed at his shrewd answer, but to me he was a symbol of the world we were moving into—a world centuries behind the Western world, where women as well as men have the right to be individuals.

After an almost sleepless night we packed again into our cars.

A Baluchi who was in the station wagon with the girls had been begging all the day before to be allowed to drive. Finally the driver consented. He had not been driving long when he began to feel for the first time the power that he had under his control. He stomped on the gas, clung to the wheel and hit one of the great rocks that blocked the road. The car turned over and the cavalcade ground to a halt. All three of my girls were bruised and shaken. We tried to find some shade beside our cars while a young medical student gave first aid, the men righted the car and changed the broken tire. Zahra was crying. All three of the girls were finding the Baluchistan mission an unusual hardship before we even got there.

We rolled and jolted on to Bampoor. Next time I would shorten this two-day-long ordeal by taking a plane, I decided.

The first evidence that we had reached Bampoor was crumbled sand-brick ruins. Once upon a time there had been a great fort at

Bampoor. Now parts of it were visible, especially since wind storms had blown away the top soil from around its broken walls and a not too recent cloudburst had ripped through a sharp gully and washed a part of the tower entirely free from sand. Later we would explore these ruins, perhaps, and try to place them in the history of our country. Now we pushed into the town.

Persians are accustomed to seeing poverty, rags, hunger, disease—these we have in Teheran and in Sarbandan—but we had never seen Bampoor. It is an ugly scraggly town with a few houses made of sun-dried brick, stone, or mud, not more than a dozen poor shops, a dirty little river and narrow filthy streets, crowded, because of our coming, with men and children. On one side the desert stretched away to the horizon; on the other to distant dun-colored mountains. The children on the streets were naked, or clothed only in dirty, waist-length shirts. The men wore long white robes, filthy at the hems, and on closer inspection not too clean elsewhere. Under the robes they wore white trousers cuffed at the ankles. Long scarfs were wrapped around their heads to make turbans.

I had seen such attire in Egypt; but one of the men in our car said that it showed the influence of India. Men of importance were called *sahib*, as in India. In the shops Afghanistan money was used to pay for Afghanistan goods, but still these people were proud to call themselves Persians.

All of my life I had seen the women of Iran wrapped from head to feet in the chadar; never had I seen Iranian men in anything but Western clothing, except, perhaps, at a village festival. These white robes seemed to thrust the culture backward several hundred years.

There were no women on the streets, another evidence of the position of women in this desert land.

"Where are the beggars?" Pooran asked, bobbling along at my elbow and finding it hard to manage her smart high heels on the broken street.

"There are none," I answered. This was hard to believe, but there were no shadows lurking in the entranceways of the naked shops, no whining ones who pushed boldly along beside us on the crumbling street.

Dr. Birjandi came out to greet us as we walked toward the sun-baked brick government compound. "Why are there no beggars in a city so poor?" I asked as soon as we had exchanged the usual Iranian pleasantries.

"These people are poor," he agreed. "Very poor. A special team studying the economic condition of Bampoor declared that Bampoor is the poorest city in the whole world. The average income is sixteen dollars a year, and the average worth of family possessions is less than one dollar. But everyone is poor together. The gendarme can carry a bag of money through the streets in safety, because there are no thieves."

No thieves and no beggars, but there were hunger and disease and all of the other ills that flock toward poverty as vultures follow dying men across the desert sands. "I must study Bampoor and the villages that are near," I told him. "I must learn for myself what needs to be done."

"Research Bampoor, Najmeh," he said quietly, "and I hope that your heart has grown hard enough so that it will not break; but do not go alone from village to village."

"This I have always done," I insisted.

"But here you could be stolen and—"

I laughed, for Dr. Birjandi often jokes. But he was serious. "This is true, Najmeh. Women are seized here and sold in Kuwait and other places where there are many men and no women."

"And still the gendarme can walk in safety with a bag of money through the streets past starving people."

"The bandits are not of Bampoor, nor of the villages. They are foreigners engaged in this smuggling."

"I saw no women on the streets of Bampoor."

"You will never see women on the streets. But often girls and women help their fathers or their husbands by following the sheep. Being a shepherdess is a lonely task, one girl with only sheep to guard her. These are the girls the bandits seize."

"I will not go alone," I promised.

One of the young engineers who had been standing near offered to take me to the first village in his jeep. But always I had found that the confidence of the people is stronger if I go among them walking. Hurriedly I put on my long full cotton skirt, my head scarf, the blouse with the high neck and long sleeves, and the gloves which I always wear in the villages. Together Pooran, the young engineer and I walked toward the nearest village, a group of black tents huddled together on the windswept plain. I knew that there were people in the tents but no one came forward to greet us.

"Tomorrow I shall visit the village and talk to the women."

The young engineer turned back toward Bampoor. "Do you speak Baluchi?"

Baluchi! One of the dialects both like and unlike the Farsi of most of Iran. In the dialects of the remote tribes the Indo-European root words are still maintained. Baluchi. Almost a new language. This I must learn since talking to women through an interpreter is like speaking through a veil.

The next morning, since meetings of the social workers who had come to Bampoor were scheduled for all day, I started out early. For a few minutes I felt as if I were walking in one of those strange dreams where the neighborhood is familiar but one's own house is missing. The black tents had disappeared. The tent village, some time during the night, had been folded up and moved away. This was a problem I had not counted on as I had lain on my bed the night before piling up the obstacles that I would have to surmount.

Dr. Birjandi had placed my girls and me in charge of feeding the fifty social workers. The supplies were already purchased and there was a cook in the kitchen, but to the cook many of the materials that had been delivered were strange and he did not know how to prepare them. The tastes of these engineers, social workers, agricultural experts from all over Iran were unknown to him. I must discuss menus with him, methods of food preparation, amounts of food to be prepared. After I had organized the morning's activities in the kitchen and set the girls to work making our quarters in the government compound cleaner and more attractive, I slipped into the first policy-making meeting. Dr. Birjandi had brought these men, experts in several fields, together to agree on *one* program, and on *one* method of reaching the people. Meeting with the fifty who had come in our caravan were those who had already been working in Bampoor—the agricultural experts who had been in the area five years studying the problems of irrigation and experimenting with fast-growing trees, and the medics who had tried to begin a disease-prevention program. My going into the meeting cut off all speaking. Whatever had been under discussion was dropped while nearly all of the men looked at me and then looked away. I had talked briefly with one of the engineers the evening we were in Zahedan. He had spent many years in America and was married to an American medical doctor who was now practicing in Iran. He did not speak but fixed me with his eyes and let one lid drop in a slow encouraging wink.

Dr. Birjandi introduced me. "This is Najmeh Najafi. She is experienced in social work. She will head our woman's program here in Baluchistan."

One of the men got to his feet. "A woman's program. I never heard of such a thing." He was simply saying what many were thinking.

Another stood. "Let us close the woman's program. There is too much of value to be done to spend time with women."

I could not blame these men. Their mothers, like mine, were at home, their chadars drawn over their faces in the presence of men who were not of their family. Their wives, though freed from the chadar, were concerned with managing beautiful homes, spoiling their children, and dressing attractively to visit or to receive visitors. I knew my country so I did not blame these men for resenting a woman sitting with them in a policy meeting.

"Gentlemen," Dr. Birjandi said, "let us go on with the discussion."

So the men accepted me, though not completely, and I kept quiet unless someone appealed to me for a bit of information, or perhaps a suggestion. When the meetings were over, for a few hours I and my girls were careful not to intrude upon the man talk; but some of the men invited themselves to our quarters in the compound for tea. Already the girls had made our sitting room look attractive.

Our first glimpse of the women of Bampoor and the villages was in the evening when we showed an educational film to a large and curious crowd. The best means of education with the backward people of my country are the strip films and the motion pictures. These have been prepared not only by the government but by experts in American Aid and by such organizations as the Near East Foundation. The picture showed how babies should be cared for— washed and soothed each day instead of being wrapped in swaddling clothes, tied tightly and left wrapped for a month or more. It also showed women busy with food preparation, with care of older children, with their own cleansing and grooming. The women, who had never seen a motion picture in their lives, were enthusiastic about this feature film.

The next night we showed pictures about sanitation and hygiene and the third night the picture was about irrigation and farming methods. After each picture we encouraged the men and women—if they dared speak up—to discuss what they had seen, to ask questions, to disagree with what the men and women in the picture were doing. I found that Baluchi would not be too difficult for me to understand since it had developed from the same Aryan roots that are the foundation of Farsi. Dr. Birjandi, of course, and two or three of the other men, were expert at the language. We hoped to find out what the people were ready to accept and use. I had learned, and so had the others, that until a man or woman is ready to receive there is no value in giving.

Our conference lasted for eight days. In these days we decided what parts of the program should come first and what should be secondary. We decided where to put the emphasis in our program and each tried to see how his part of the work fitted into the entire program. At the end of the eight days Dr. Birjandi returned to his work as general director of these programs for all Iran and we were left to bring a new day, a new life, to Baluchistan.

I enjoyed the conference, but still I could not wait until it was finished to try to see the women in their own tents, to begin the careful research on which I would base my program.

The day the conference ended I saw an old woman sitting alone under a palm tree. I walked toward her to ask for words of wisdom. In my country the young often ask for wisdom from the aged. But as I walked toward her the woman died. Without a word, with just a long agonized look of one who is afraid to face the unknown, her head fell forward, her body slumped away from the tree trunk and she lay huddled like a heap of rags.

I had met the young doctor who was assigned to our program. I hurried to him and was angry when he shrugged and said, "She is one of many."

"But why?" I insisted.

"Under the city of Bampoor there are large water storage basins. The water is not fit to drink, but these people insist on drinking it. They die of a disease called *bapouk*. There is no cure for this disease."

"And there is no other water for drinking?"

"There is this weak stream called a river that runs through Bampoor. There is the River Haraband. The river water, too, is contaminated." I turned away, but now I knew that my first project with the women would be to help them to find pure water for themselves and their families.

I turned back to the doctor. "Can this water be purified with perchlorine?" In the village of Sarbandan I had taught the villagers to put perchlorine in the drinking water. Some of them had objected at first but I had refused to care for their children in the clinic, and they had cooperated.

"Perchlorine would help, but it is not enough. First the water must be filtered."

"Teach me how." I sat down upon the floor of the clinic and waited for him to begin the explanation.

"You are in haste," he told me, but he brought out some clay bowls and some chalk. He showed me how the water could filter through the chalk from one bowl to the next and come out cleansed. "But you must not push this thing. If you do you will undo all that we have tried to start here."

"We will go slowly, slowly," I promised. But already I was dreaming of pure water in every tent.

After the conference ended Dr. Birjandi remained for a time to supervise putting the project in motion, but I was free to go ahead planning and carrying out the woman's program. Of course we began with patient instruction on how to filter water, and of course the women were reluctant to give up drinking from their water basins and from the rivers. A swamp spread along the low bank of the river. It was not my duty to drain the swamp over the objection of the people. The men and women clung to the swamp because it was a bit of life in the dryness of the desert; because the eye could rest on the greenness from the sharp radiance of the sand. It was my duty to explain why these silent waters must be drained, to tell the story of malaria so often that these people would begin to understand.

I had known that work in Baluchistan would be difficult—but I had not known the strength of the wall that these primitive people would build against us. They felt that they had no need for us; that we were intruders. For centuries without number they had managed without the aid of "foreigners." It would take all of our imagination and persistence to find an opening for ourselves.

Dr. Birjandi, since he had been all over Baluchistan by camel, knew the needs of the people, and he knew their nature as well. If he said that something I had planned to try would not work, I gave up the plan. I, myself, couldn't see the woman's work apart from the master plan which had been developed and was being put into effect by Italconsult. In Sarbandan I had gone alone into the village and had tried to advise and help both the men and women in all of their activities. Here, in Baluchistan, there were experts in each field. One young man was proficient with tools. He taught masonry, carpentry, other practical building skills. It was our hope that soon the people would move out of their tents into permanent homes. Another team worked with agriculture, the draining of swamps, the attempts to use irrigation. Already there was what we call a garden, but it was more like a nursery for trees, or even a park. Already the people had noticed that this garden modified the climate and made the temperature less impossible to live with. There was the doctor who was interested particularly in sanitation and hygiene, though he treated the sick and the injured—those who would come to him.

Then there were my girls and I, interested in interpreting the values of the whole program to the women. Sanitation must begin in the home; so must health habits. In agriculture the woman works beside the man; she must know why the man is doing what he does, why he is doing it in the way he is doing it. Education, too, begins in the home, and if we were to reduce the illiteracy by the slightest point the women would need to be converted to sending their children to school. Always before, as a social worker, I had considered the women's program as something almost separate from other development programs. In Bampoor I saw that it was a part of every program.

The girls and I began our work as I had in Sarbandan. In simple clothes and with no make-up on our faces, we went among the women walking. At first they sat silently, almost sullenly, before us. It was little Pooran, whose hunched back excited their sympathy and whose courage excited their admiration, who first reached them. In some mystic way she sensed their need while the rest of us sought only to discover it through words.

The women knew nothing about sanitation—nothing. They never bathed, though sometimes they got wet when they forded rivers. They never had bathed. Moslems must wash a part of their body before praying, but only a part: the feet, the hands and arms, the teeth and the gums. These women had never used a latrine—had never seen one. It was hard for me to remember that they had always been on the move; going to the mountains, coming from the mountains, staying only a brief time in the high valleys or on the low plains. To build and use permanent latrines would have been impossible. But now the government hoped that they would settle down and stay near Bampoor. They must learn not to contaminate the area in which they lived. So we began to tell of the latrine. How it is built, how it is used, how it is kept sanitary.

In many parts of Asia there has been, always, a shortage of wood. Where there is a shortage of wood a floor civilization develops. People do not sit on chairs because there is no wood for chairs. In the same way in much of Asia the latrine is a floor installation. In the simplest form there is a trench dug and a stone is placed on each side on which one puts his feet. A more sophisticated Asian latrine is made with a concrete bowl, open at the bottom, set in a slab of concrete. This is called a sanitary slab, and it has the advantage of cutting down the number of flies that inhabit an open trench. The women of Baluchistan, accustomed to stopping anywhere on the desert or in the fields, had to be taught that there was a better way.

Iranians use the aftabe, a narrow-necked jug with a handle on the side which holds water for a special purpose. People who do not use tissue in the latrine carry it with them for cleansing purposes.

The women of Baluchistan knew nothing about water for personal cleansing. They used a convenient rock picked up from the field. Just to introduce the aftabe would be difficult.

The women, during their periods, sat upon the ground for three or four days, letting the earth absorb the flow of blood. In this way had the women of Genesis in the Old Testament met this need. Using sanitary napkins would be a major change in their lives.

So much to be taught, so much to be learned, and no one really eager to change her way of life. I thought often of my first months in Sarbandan. There the women had brought their children willingly to the clinic, there they had sent their girls, and come themselves, to hear of sanitation and health while they learned to use the needle and the loom. Here nothing that we taught seemed to touch the women's desire to learn. We must be patient, patient. Sometime, for some reason, the women would come to us. And because we had to move so slowly we sometimes felt that we were moving backward. Yet we weren't. We were learning how nomads live. And before long if we worked with love and not in haste we would learn from the women their customs, their legends, their sorrows, their hopes and dreams.

The women were reluctant to invite us into their tents, though after a time they were willing to come outside and sit with us on the sand in the tent's shade, and we never entered any tent without an invitation. In Sarbandan I had stood by the gelim-covered doors and called, "Who-oo. Anybody home?" and most of the women had invited me to a tea. Here the women listened to our talking, sometimes responding with a sound in the throat, sometimes smiling a little. It is a happiness to see a smile come into the eyes or even onto the lips of a woman whose face is usually somber. Sometimes we drank tea with the women, being grateful that water must be boiled for tea. One day Fahti, a woman more pleasant and a little more bold than the others, brought out a ja-jim for us to sit upon.

"This is so beautiful," I said, touching the rough wool of the Persian blanket with a praising finger. And speaking in my limited Baluchi, "Do you have a loom?"

"We have the loom," she said. "Tomorrow we shall make a loom for you to see."

So the next day we went to Fahti's tent and outdoors in the shade she set up her loom. The loom was six pieces of wood placed flat on the ground, two by two and at a distance of five meters. There was a young bride in the tent of the mother-in-law and she was just learning to thread the loom. Threading was a long process and finally Fahti helped her with incredibly quick, practiced hands. These women have skillful hands, I thought. Perhaps through their hands they will find a better life.

And I thought of Sarbandan and the hand looms we had set up in our schoolroom and of the dream that was always with me to make of Sarbandan a weaving center if only someday I could find help in building and equipping a factory.

While I thought of Sarbandan I watched the women, sitting on the ground and weaving a product as even and tight as if they had a sophisticated loom.

Pooran and I asked to be taught how to weave on this loom and the women blushed with pleasure. It is easier to teach one who has taught you. There is an equality that makes learning not a cure for ignorance that is embarrassing but an exchange that is noble.

Now that Fahti had shown her confidence in us, the other women were braver and more open. Two young women invited us to watch them make the straw and palm-frond mats that serve as carpets in the tents of the poor. Another told us that her husband was a maker of boats. With two of the engineers we watched the boat-making. The very small boats are called *toutean* and they are used for traveling and fishing on Hamoun Lake.

Still the women were reluctant to open their tents to us.

One morning as Zahra and I were walking toward one of the more distant villages we heard a halloo and, turning, saw Fahti standing beside her tent and waving to us to come nearer.

I was a little surprised. Zahra tried with all of her heart to do the work we had set for ourselves, but her wrinkling nose with its bridge of freckles, her youthful spirits, even the way she walked with a special tossing of her body, seemed to disturb the Baluchi women. But now we two were being invited to some special thing.

"Come into the tent," Fahti said, lifting the ja-jim over the opening. I could feel my blood beating heavily in my head. I now let myself think that I had been afraid that we would never be accepted into the tents and inner lives of the people.

For a moment we could not see in the darkness. Under our feet was the coarse palm-frond mat. We could see along the edges of the tent the goatskins that hold flour, yogurt, seed, other supplies. Fahti lifted the ja-jim again and secured it so that a panel of light fell through the tent. In the center was a young girl in a blue chiffon dress. The married Baluchi women always dress in black, the unmarried women in red or sometimes in cotton prints. Never had I seen blue chiffon in Baluchistan.

"She is a bride," Fahti said. "You must see her before she puts on the white veil."

"Beautiful," we said. "Beautiful." The girl's dark hair was oiled until it shone and the ends had been passed through pierced Afghanistan coins. Coins hung from her ears, and, most surprising, a ring had been passed through her nose. The ring was of gold and the bride seemed to be happy to have it there. Zahra knew no reluctance when she was curious. She wrinkled her nose and eyes in surprise. "Why does a girl so young have a ring in the nose?"

Fahti answered, "A ring is for the nose of the woman. Even a small boy can handle a stubborn camel if there is a ring in the nose. Even a new husband can handle a stubborn wife."

The girl's feet were bare. But then ninety percent of the Baluchistan people are barefooted. Most of the others wrap the feet in strips of hide in a sort of crude sandal. While we watched, Fahti put the white scarf over the girl's head and brought out the marriage coat— an intricately made garment of red and black. It was not until the bride stepped into the full panel of light that we noticed that on her forehead there was a mark such as the women of India wear. Another evidence of a close relationship to the neighbors on the east.

We hoped to be invited to the marriage ceremony, but as abruptly as Fahti had opened herself to us she again closed herself away. She offered us another cup of tea and we knew that we were again strangers.

Back at headquarters we talked about the bride and wondered about the marriage customs. Even the engineers who had been in Baluchistan the longest knew little of the really intimate traditions of the people. It was some time before Pooran heard this story and brought it home to us.

The camel—which in Baluchistan has two humps—is a sacred animal. It is only the camel that is worthy to be traded for a wife. The marriage brokers are usually old women who must know camels as well as boys and girls. Most marriages are arranged for girls in their middle teens and to live with one's own family after the age of twenty is indeed a sad thing.

There is a peculiar custom—important of course to the old women who operate their marriage businesses in this way—which makes the selection of a husband seem more the work of Allah than of a village matchmaker.

The month of Ramazan is with all Moslems a holy month since we believe that God revealed most of the Koran during this month. The people of Baluchistan call the last day of this month of fasting and prayer "Farewell Friday." On this day the unmarried girls who feel themselves ready for marriage rise before dawn and go from the east gate of the city to the Mosque of Zebarband. The mosque has two doors. The unmarried girls, accompanied by an ancient kinswoman—either the matchmaker or an accomplice, perhaps—go in at the east door. The girl, following the instructions of the old woman, unbuttons any button on her clothing, unhooks any hook, unlaces any lacing. She even takes off her earrings. When there is no closed thing on her body the girl sits with her feet folded under her, her forehead on the ground, and prays a special prayer. When the prayer is finished the old woman buttons every button, hooks every hook, ties every lace. Then she leads the girl, now with closed eyes, out of the mosque by the west door. At this door young men are waiting or walking (by previous arrangement, of course). The old woman stops one of the young men. She knows why he is here and no doubt he does also, but there is supposed to be uncanny second sight in the old woman's stopping the right man. The girl opens her eyes, the boy leaves his companions to guide her to the mosque and this opens the way for acquaintance and marriage.

Of course, this little play, staged by the matchmaker, is only a play, but many of the young men and girls more than half believe that in this way the mate that is exactly right for them can be selected. Are not a mosque and a prayer part of the whole incident?

What the people really believe is that the whole future of a marriage depends upon how faithfully the actual marriage ceremony customs are followed. If a girl wants a husband who will always be faithful to her, who will never divorce her, who will beat her only when it is for her own good, she must follow the pattern in every detail.

For the ceremony the bride is seated with her feet on a white towel. Under the towel there is salt. Civilization, the nomads know, must follow not only water, but salt. The bride's eyes are upon an open Koran. She is supposed to be reading, but of course she cannot read the Arabic. Very few Baluchi women can read even their own language. Now one of the old kinswomen takes a silk string and makes a knot in it for each of the groom's relatives. Thus their mouths are tied and they will never be able to criticize the bride. In a dish there is a mixture of yogurt and dry clay brought from a sacred shrine. The bride puts her finger in this mixture, then in her mouth. This will secure for her a happy relationship with her husband. After she rises, the towel is taken up and the salt is carefully collected. This will be used for cooking, and the food prepared with it will make the groom prosperous.

It often seemed to us that all of these charms fail. The position of women—illustrated by the ring in the nose, even though the ring may be made of silver or gold or even set with jewels—is unthinkable, even to us Iranian women who have never, until very recently, been considered equal to men. It is the usual thing for men to beat their wives; and once a gendarme found a woman who had been chained in a cave for ten years because her husband was so jealous that he feared she would be unfaithful to him.

The life of a Baluchi woman is hard. She works side by side with her man; she follows the yearly migrations, bearing a part of the burden, assisting in herding the animals, and all the time she is carrying a child lashed to her back in a sort of wooden cradle and another yet unborn.

But there is pleasure too, laughter and music. The Baluchi musical instruments are a kind of drum shaped like a cylinder which hangs from the neck, a mandolin-type six-stringed instrument often played with a bow, and a flute made of cane or bamboo or wood. At times the music is hauntingly beautiful, at other times rhythmical and boisterous, filled with freedom and the energy that makes it possible for these people to keep alive under the hardships that press upon them.

It was our problem to reduce those hardships without curtailing the freedom and vigor of spirit. But deep inside myself I knew that I could do nothing until I could reach the souls of these women whose life touched mine only on the outside edges.

We were eager to conduct classes, eager to teach a better way of life, but to us the women were distant. Only Fahti had opened her door to us and then just briefly. Really she seemed frightened by her own overtures—or her husband had cautioned her—for now she seemed to be avoiding us.

There were ways to force these women to us, but I wanted them to come eagerly and of their own will.

One day I stopped with Pahvine to watch the making of bread. The wheat had already been washed, dried in the sun, and ground to a coarse flour. Salt and water had been added, too, and now one of the women, sitting flat on the ground, was mixing it, kneading it, shaping it into a loaf. We watched as her quick brown hands caressed the dough with strength and assurance. She soon set it aside and covered it with a cloth. "It will sour now," Pahvine said. The woman, who had paid little attention to us, raised her eyes and said, "If no man looks upon it and no one touches it, it will become larger. Much larger."

We thanked her for allowing us to watch her and surprisingly she said, "I am Ashraf. You may stay until it rises." We sat down beside her and talked of the food that her family ate. "Dates are good," she said. "Even when one is so poor as to have only the pits, dates are good."

"Bread is better," Pahvine said, and Ashraf agreed. "Bread is everything."

The poor, she told us, live on wild grass and weeds and the pits of the dates. In the spring when the plants are green and tender the children are sent into the field to graze with the animals. But for her family she always had bread, yogurt, cheese, and fish from the lake.

We walked on and sought conversation with other women outside their tents. When we returned Ashraf had divided the loaf into buns and set them to rise. "Do not count these breads," Ashraf told us. "Some will disappear if you count them."

"I myself have never heard of this," I said.

Ashraf nodded vigorously. "It is true. This I have seen happen." She called two of her children (children who should be in school, I thought) to help her to gather weeds to make a fire for the baking of the bread. Over the fire she put a flat metal tray and on the tray she put the buns, carefully flattened. When the bread was baked the aroma made this wilderness a home like any other home in the world where love and care bake fresh-risen bread.

"We thank you for teaching us how to make the bread," I said. "We would like to return your kindness. Will you come to our school and let us teach you to make the cookie as a special treat for your family?"

"I can make the taushak," she said. This is a sort of bun with sugar and perhaps nuts added to the bread dough.

"We make the reshteh-b-reshteh from rice," I said, "and the elephant ears from wheat flour and egg and butter." She folded and unfolded her hands but made no answer. "These things we have in our kitchen," we said. "Sometime perhaps we can have a party with fried garbanzos mixed with raisins, dried apricots, peaches, pears and mulberries."

Perhaps she had never heard of elephant ears or reshteh-b-reshteh, a crisp delicious cookie that isn't known to the West. Perhaps fruit had been for her only a dream, but still she hesitated. "Such food is for the rich," she protested. But finally she said, "I will come."

When she came she brought Fahti and the young bride with her. The next day three others came. We could begin to hold classes. Sometimes we held our class outside in the shade of some building, sometimes in a tent. The women who had sat upon the ground all of their lives felt comfortable in this sort of "classroom." The first brave ones brought a few others. Our class was not large but it was a wedge in the wall that the Baluchi women had built against us. All of our teaching was done through showing. "In this way we cleanse the baby," Pooran or Pahvine might say. Their slow-moving hands going through the process step by step under the eyes of the women were the real teachers. "In this way we make the water clean so that death does not hide in it," I might say, and then in the same slow, careful way my hands would move to demonstrate the simple process. Always there was some food as a special treat.

We had made a beginning, but only a beginning. Though we could still feel the hostility of our students I had to leave the girls to conduct the classes while I turned my attention to other problems.

In Bampoor and in the villages that surround the city, there are two distinct classes: the rich and the poor. The rich would seem poor in any other society, but in comparison with most of the Baluchi people they are well off indeed. They own the camels, the sheep and the goats. They gather some wealth by selling the sheep and the goats, and by renting the camels.

Now, in Bampoor, there is a third class—the government employees. At first the coming of these people made little difference since the chasm between these newcomers and the nomadic Baluchi was so great that there was no bridge between. But imperceptibly things began to change. Always the people had been satisfied with their lot; if there were problems they took them to their kadkhoda. But now there was a growing restlessness in the town. For the first time there were thefts of money, boats, store goods. Was it well to trade the peace of the people for water, electricity, schools, soap, play equipment, a tractor with a trained driver? Is it better to be content in a black tent or seething with envy and discontent in a new home where there are food and medical care? Though the men were filled with talk of electricity, water and schools, the women seemed reluctant to move into a disquieting life. Only by moving slowly, and very slowly, could we give them the new, without taking from them the old.

One day I stopped to visit with Fahti for a moment as she came for water. Often I had looked at the robes of the women, but today Fahti's robe interested me especially. It was new. Under the neckline in front was a small patch of exquisite embroidery; because the robe was new the colors in this very fine work were brilliant and the design stood out sharply. "That is a beautiful design."

"Always we have had it," she answered.

The design was traditional, then. "Are all embroideries alike?" I asked.

"Many we have always."

I began really to look at the women's robes. Each robe had a small area of embroidery in the same place. The designs differed, but I soon realized that they were all repeats, with individual variations, of a few basic patterns.

Although my budget was extremely low and my own salary was barely a fourth of what I would be paid in America for similar work, I began to trade new robes for old so that I could study and reproduce these designs. I was the wicked wizard of "Aladdin and the Wonderful Lamp" who went through the streets crying, "New lamps for old, new lamps for old." What I had found was as exciting as the magic lamp which Aladdin's wife unknowingly traded for a useless one.

Though men may not believe this, I had found in my work that men give women a higher place in society if the women are productive in some way that men can appreciate. A woman is expected to bear and rear a family, to keep the home together, to do half the work in the fields, to provide the family with food and clothing—it is only when she goes beyond these expected tasks that the husband's interest in her as a person is challenged.

The women who embroidered these robes were more clever with their needles than anyone I had ever known. I thought of the women of Sarbandan struggling to learn the simplest stitches. The thread these women used was finer than spool silk and the embroidery pattern covered the material so completely that no cloth was visible. The wedding coat which I had thought was red and black was in reality all black except for the bindings. The red was the predominant color in the embroidery. Would the women like to embroider for the school? They would be paid twenty-five cents a day. These women had never earned a penny in their lives. They had worked with their husbands but they had never had the use of any of the income. Twenty-five cents was to them real riches! This, in comparison with their family income, was about the same as a hundred dollars to an American housewife.

One at a time the women came to our school. They came barefoot. One woman came from a distant village and brought a loaf of bread to last for a week. She returned by foot to spend Friday with her family and bake another loaf of bread.

For the first time the women of the tribe were open to us. While they embroidered we could talk to them of sanitation, of nutrition. Not all of the women, of course, but I knew that soon . . .

We had come in April and now it was late June. The nomads, always in the high valleys before this time, grew restless, eager to be on their way. They would leave behind them men to care for the newly started gardens. The government had hoped that the mass of people would be willing to stay in one place; but we realized that to force them now would be to undo much that we had done.

It was incredible how fast the black tents of the six villages folded. How abruptly the city of Bampoor closed its eyes against the summer sun.

"You should not do my shopping in the middle of the day," I told my servant, Rigi. "The sun will melt you."

He laughed as he set his groceries on the floor. "Once upon a time it was hot here. That was before the planting of trees."

I fanned myself with my account book. "What do people do when summer really comes?"

"There are many ways of outwitting the heat. In the evening when the sun is gone we gather thorns from the desert. These we pile in front of the house, first discovering which way the wind is blowing. We pour water on the thorns and the wind coming over the water becomes a mild breeze flavored with the smell of thorn."

"And other ways?" I asked him.

Abruptly his good-natured face disintegrated into a fit of mirth. When he could speak again he said, "In the old days, before the planting of trees, the government agents did not wear clothing— only very short cotton pants and hardly that." Again he fell into a fit of laughter. "Lady Najafi, you will please forgive me, but when this picture comes back to me . . ." Finally he told me that behind each desk there was a big terra cotta jar of water in which the men would sit while they did their day's work. There was one man—the boss—who had such an outsized abdomen that he could fit into his jar only by lifting it over the edge of the jar. One day a new officer, transferred from Azerbaijan, where even the summers were cool, came looking for the boss. He really got shocked when he found the boss was the big naked man in the big terra cotta jar. And then Rigi finished, "But it didn't take long for this young man to find himself a jar."

Rigi set about putting the food away. He did this with a flourish —to be the janitor of the office and a personal servant besides— what status! "You will not have to find yourself a jar, Lady Najafi," he said. "I, personally, will gather thorns for you; and besides it is cooler, much cooler, with the trees."

My laughing servant was disappointed when I told him that I would need neither thorns nor a jug. The workers in the development department were to return to Teheran for the hottest months. We would not come back until the nomads came down from the mountains in the fall.

Now that there was little we could do in Bampoor I was eaten up with eagerness to return to Teheran. Mother had written that Sina was putting words together to make sentences, was learning to say "no" with some regularity and that he was interested in and curious about everything. Nassim was turning herself over, trying to sit up, and becoming a real little person. If only Shapoor were in Teheran! He wrote enthusiastic, happy letters about his courses in history, in international current problems and in international relations. When we had planned to go to America we had thought that Shapoor would be interested in taking social science courses, or perhaps business or community administration, but his interest was turning to government. He missed me, of course, but he was very busy. I missed him, especially at times when the work was going slowly, when some specially frustrating incident had occurred. He had a gentle, almost inarticulate way of reaching out toward me by tousling my hair, running a finger under my chin or across an eyebrow. Such little things grow big when they are missed!

In Teheran I would stay in my mother's home long enough to greet my brothers and sisters, and then with my babies I would go to Sarbandan. I thought of the village with the cherries and apricots already ripe for the harvest, of Mash'hadi Mokhtar, the capitalist of the village with his shining gold teeth, perhaps bought from a tray in the goldsmith's street of the bazaar, of the tall Kadkhoda, of the men and women and boys and girls who were so close to me. The summer would be short but I had fine plans for Sarbandan.

And at night I felt the warmth of Nassim against me and saw the merry face of Sina when were again together.

When the autumn came we would return to Bampoor, but with much of our learning behind us we would know how to give to the Baluchi nomads without taking from them. The women would have an opportunity to use their skill with the needle to free themselves from want. We would walk easily over the bridge that God would help us to build.

4 ❧ Summer in Sarbandan

SUMMER IS NOT THE MOST PLEASANT SEASON OF THE YEAR IN Iran—yet there is something about the blueness of the sky, the special vital quality of the sunlight, that makes the heart respond to an unearthly beauty. Perhaps to see this one must be deeply Persian; to the Persian the sunlight is a kind of liquid music. Even Bampoor, lying naked on the dun-colored plain, is bathed in this peculiar vibrant light. As our plane lifted from the sands and circled above Bampoor a horizontal layer of light came between us and the city and it no longer looked ragged and hungry. Instead it looked as peaceful as a golden cat, relaxing and stretching in the sun.

Although my eyes, my arms, were hungry for my children, although my heart jumped with eagerness to be again in Sarbandan, my village, still I clung to this sleeping city with dreams and plans for my return.

In Teheran there was much to do: social things like sitting with my sisters, my friends, with tea glasses cupped in our hands, discussing, perhaps, the latest fashions; mothering things like bathing and dressing my little ones, singing to Nassim and telling stories to Sina; routine domestic things like employing Ramazan, the bright-eyed boy from Sarbandan, to be my servant and his aunt to be the children's nurse; business things like reporting the progress of the Baluchistan Woman's Program to the government agency and filing a careful list of the materials needed for the next year's program.

Finally the business was completed. "We will take the children to Sarbandan," I told my family and my mother added, "I will go with Najmeh."

"Dear Mother, certainly." To me we were one family: Mother, Sina, Nassim and myself. Tardily I thought of Shapoor. When Shapoor had finished his education in America the family would open its tight little wall and make room for him.

Sarbandan!

When I had been working with the Near East Foundation I had developed a philosophy of social work that was all my own. I hoped to work heart by heart, not in the mechanized way that I had found large organizations must move. I did not want to make a little America in the mountains of Persia. I wanted my people to stay as they were, keeping the feeling of security that is born of doing things in the traditional way. I wanted to see if a better way of life could be built upon a foundation of native customs and traditions. For my people I wanted happiness and the fulfillment of their own dreams.

And so I had talked with Mash'hadi Mokhtar about the village of Sarbandan.

Mash'hadi Mokhtar was the wealthiest man in the village. He owned the teahouse, the bus line between Teheran and Sarbandan, wheat land, garden land and orchards. I sat in his teahouse, where usually only men drank tea together or smoked their pipes in communal silence. He was uneasy to have a woman guest but I spoke without embarrassment.

"Who owns this village?" I had asked.

"Some landlords. A few big ones. I am one of these." And his gold teeth had glittered under his magnificent mustache.

"What about the population of Sarbandan?"

"Almost two thousand in the summer."

"And in the winter?"

"When there is no work there is no food."

"The winters are long?"

He gestured toward the inner room of the teahouse. "See, we still have the khorsee." Three old men sat in the teahouse with their legs covered with a blanket spread over a stool that held it above a small charcoal fire. The khorsee is the center of warmth in all humble Iranian homes.

"How do people live through such a long cold winter?"

"They go to Mazandaran. They work in the rice fields. Only women and children remain in Sarbandan."

We talked for a time, then I asked, "Do you have a bath?"

"Bath? How could we have? Our fathers made one about a hundred years ago, but it is ruined now. Its pool is so unclean that no one has a desire to go into it."

"Do you have a school, Mashdi Mokhtar?"

"Indeed we do. Four years ago we built a school. We have grades one, two, three, and four. Next year, perhaps we will have five and six. If not next year at least some year."

"And is there a school for girls?"

"What are you talking about, my lady? A school for girls!"

"Tell me, does Sarbandan have a clinic?"

"Clinic? What is this clinic?"

"A place for the care of the sick."

"How could we have such a place when there is no doctor?"

Then I had followed Mash'hadi Mokhtar through the village. I had seen women washing clothes on both sides of the jube, farther up a man killing a lamb and the lamb's blood running into the stream. And between the lamb and the washing stones—a young girl lifting a dripping jug of household water to her shoulder. I had seen that the village needed me. That night I had returned to my sister Fahkri's home and said, "I think I have found my village." And she had said, "Najmeh-jun. You are very crazy."

But I had not been crazy. I had rented a house and had modernized it for living quarters and for a school for the girls and women. The village council had met often and had cooperated in building a bathhouse, a clinic, a room for the washing of the dead. The women had built a latrine for the men near the village mosque, and many villagers had prepared a place for a sanitary latrine slab, given to them as a gift if they would make use of it.

All of my dreams for Sarbandan had not yet come true. The women had learned to put perchlorine in their household water, they had learned to wash their clothes away from the stream that provided drinking water. They had come, of their own choosing, to the clinic and to the school. Still the village was poor. Still most of the men had to leave during the winter months for the rice fields of Mazandaran. There was much yet to be accomplished.

I thought that I should, perhaps, go ahead of my family, Mother, Sina, and Nassim, and make arrangements for us all. There are two ways to get to Sarbandan from Teheran. Recently the road had been improved, which made the two-hour drive in a private car almost comfortable. And then there was the bus. The bus line is privately owned: Mash'hadi Mokhtar owns it and his brothers drive it. It leaves Teheran any time that the passengers arrive at the terminal, and gets to Sarbandan any time that is convenient to the driver. On the bus there is much merrymaking. Most of the time some passenger sits on an up-ended box near the driver and entertains with a continuous story. Persians love the tall tale, and since most of these stories are shouted at top voice everyone on the bus laughs, scoffs, or adds to the story.

I would go by bus, I decided, and I would take Pooran with me. But Mohsen had other ideas. He would take all of us in his car; though the trip might not be so gay at least it would be safe.

We filled the car and we were nearly as gay and as crowded as we would have been on the bus. Mother had Nassim on her lap and was singing bits of songs she had sung to me in my baby days; Pooran chattered eagerly of the people she had learned to love when she was a young girl, living with me and learning to teach others as she herself studied and learned; Sina hugged very close the great brown teddy bear he had carried with him all the way from America. I carried several towels to care for Sina when the curving road brought the carsickness. And Mohsen drove, of course. Ramazan and Nannie had gone ahead by bus, carrying all of their own belongings and much of the household material we would need for a long visit.

The samovar was bubbling in many homes even before we drove into Sarbandan. In the homes of the tall Kadkhoda and of Ramazan's parents there were dried apricot pits and watermelon seeds as well as glasses of hot tea. Everyone wanted to admire Sina and Nassim and say "Salaam" to my mother. It was only at the teahouse of Mash'hadi Mokhtar that I met with gloom. We sat facing each other on a strip of carpet with glasses of tea between our hands.

"Mash'hadi Mokhtar," I began, seeing the dark look in his expressive eyes, "how is Sarbandan?"

"You have seen a mud hut covered with fresh white plaster," he said, and his brown eyes grew even more grave under the magnificent overhang of his brows. "Sarbandan is such a house."

"You mean that the school, the clinic, the bath, all of these things are like a coat of whitewash applied over a crumbling house?"

He took a long sip of his tea. "Perhaps it is wrong to say this, Lady Najafi, but it is so."

For a moment I was tempted to speak out in anger. I wanted to tell this sober man that for some reason he did not appreciate the good things that he, himself, had helped to acquire for the village. Had he not given land for the clinic? Had he not supported the bathhouse? But I knew that if I spoke I would silence him. "Tell me, Mash'hadi Mokhtar, why this is so."

He put down his glass and laced his long dark fingers together. His eyes followed his fingers. "As long as there is poverty here, the real house is ancient and crumbling." He looked up at me. "I have a fine suit of clothes. Is that not so? My brothers each have a good sweater, a good shirt. Is that not so? Also the tall Kadkhoda has a good suit. Is there another good suit in the village?"

There were the doctor, the schoolteacher, but of course I did not name these. These men were not of the village; they were foreigners.

"Until every man can put by his suit of patches Sarbandan cannot take on new life. And the women. Who knows what rags are beneath the chadar."

"You have not spoken of this before. Why?"

He shrugged his shoulders, holding his open palms toward me. "I have never once asked that these hands be filled, Lady Najafi. I speak for others who are not as fortunate as I am. Listen, in the winter we can live because there is hope for the spring. In the spring there is hope that soon there will be the ripening of the cherry and the apricot. But now the cherries and the apricots have been taken to market and still the men find themselves in debt—"

"Debt is not a good thing," I agreed. "Still, has it not always been so?"

"It has always been so." He was silent as he lifted his tea glass and took another sip. "Many bad things had always been so: the death of children in summer, no school for the girls, a bathhouse fallen into rottenness. You showed us, Lady Najafi, that although a thing had long been with us we could make changes. You showed us."

Abruptly I decided that now was the time for me to make an important move. I had thought until my work in Baluchistan was completed I could wait to start a new project in Sarbandan. But Sarbandan was ready. Mash'hadi Mokhtar, Sarbandan's first citizen, had spoken.

I put aside my tea glass. "Mash'hadi Mokhtar, I have an idea. A plan."

"I will help." He went for his chopogh. Carefully he filled it, drew upon it three times, wiped the mouthpiece carefully across his cheek and passed it to me. I, too, drew upon it three times.

"We must call a meeting," I said. "This plan must be of the people."

While we were in Sarbandan my mother ran my household. Sina was having the best time of his life. The village children were not as firm with him as his cousins since Sina was a stranger and must be pampered. He was not as free as he thought he was. Ramazan, who, of course, knew everybody in the village, made sure that all was well with him and kept him under his eye all of the time. Nassim slept, wakened, played with her American plastic rattle and slept again. A better baby never lived. Even when she began to cut her first teeth she stayed well and content. I saw little of Mother, of Sina, of Nassim; I allowed myself to be submerged, to be drowned in the village, its joys and problems.

The night the Rish e safed met in my home I was, as usual, the only woman present. The men had become accustomed to me. I think they had stopped thinking of me as a woman. For a brief time we talked of the school, the clinic—all of the things that Sarbandan had acquired. I spoke few words, but each word was used to tell them that these things they had got for themselves. I had helped, yes, but mostly because I knew how to go about getting the things they needed. I was preparing them to take a new load on their shoulders, and their shoulders needed strengthening.

Finally I raised my eyes to Mash'hadi Mokhtar's and he spoke. "I have told Lady Najafi that we have better health, we have better education, but we are still poor."

"Is that not to be expected?" one old man asked with surprise. "Surely all of the villagers of Iran are poor."

"It does not need to be so," I said. "We have walked many miles together, you and I, but there are many more before us if we would leave poverty behind."

The Kadkhoda turned to me. "You know the path that walk must follow?"

"Look," I said, "I know the way, but it is a hard path." They were all quiet so I went on. "What do we have in this village that will bring us money?"

One of the men knew the answer to that question. There are no better cherries and apricots in the world than develop in the mountain valleys of Iran—and Sarbandan is the richest of these orchards. "We have the apricot and the cherry," they said.

The men waited for me to speak but I was silent. Finally the Kadkhoda said, "These we sell in Teheran. We have the better road, and the fruit reaches the market when it is fresh and unspoiled." He looked from one of the men to the other but no one spoke. "There are apricots and cherries to be eaten by ourselves and our families. There are apricots to dry for the winter and for the market."

"These you have always had and you have always been poor," I said.

One of the men shrugged and lighted his hubbly-bubbly. The sound of the water boiling made music in the quiet room.

"These we have had always," they agreed.

"If you would leave poverty behind, you must walk past those things that you have had always," I said.

Mash'hadi Mokhtar drew his enormous brows into a deep frown. "Where will we find the path that leads past poverty, Lady Najafi?"

"Have you looked closely at your own orchard?" I asked.

Musi, Mash'hadi Mokhtar's younger brother, ran his fingers between the turtleneck of his knitted cotton shirt and his bronzed skin. "Many of our trees are old. Even for us a tree will not bear forever."

I watched Mash'hadi Mokhtar's face. He could not endure having anything that he owned criticized as he considered even his wheat fields and his bus line an extension of himself. Now surprisingly he answered. "We need trees to take the place of those that die. We need to kill the insects that feed upon our trees. Some of our trees bear bitter fruit."

"There is a program in Iran to improve the orchard," I said. "There are new trees that have been tested for growing in our climate; there is instruction on how to space these trees as they do in America, to get a larger crop from each tree; there are medicines and treatments for sick trees and there is quick death for the insects that eat the tender green leaves and the worms that ruin the fruit."

The man with the hubbly-bubbly laid aside the mouthpiece. "Are these given to us, Lady Najafi?"

"Not given," I told them. "We have already learned that nothing of value is given. These things we can buy—" I watched the expression on their concerned faces, "—with borrowed money."

I had now spoken the frightening word. There is scarcely a villager who has not sold himself into a kind of slavery through borrowing money. In villages where landlords have owned the earth, the water, the animals, the seed, many farmers have lived all of their lives on "next year's" earnings. Never have they been free to leave the landlord or seek personal betterment. In villages like Sarbandan where there are many landlords, perhaps captivity has been to the local shopkeepers, for weddings and funerals must be properly celebrated even when there is no money available for rice and shoes. My eyes went to Mash'hadi Mokhtar's face. So recently he had spoken to me of the weight of this debt that is never lifted, and I had agreed, "Debt is a bad thing."

"There is another kind of borrowing," I said, praying that I could make the difference clear to them. "In this borrowing no man is alone. Instead we all make a study of what the village needs to lift us from poverty. Do we need trees, insecticides, poultry, wheat for planting, even a tractor to make our unirrigated wheat land profitable? We study all of our needs and then we form a cooperative and borrow together."

No one spoke and I asked, "What have you done since Mr. Malak Mansoor was here?"

Before Shapoor and I had left Iran for our year in America, even before we had left our home in Sarbandan, Mr. Malak Mansoor, head of cooperatives in Iran, had visited Sarbandan. All of the villagers had gathered to hear him speak. He had explained the advantages of the cooperative.

Now the Kadkhoda spoke. "We have thought about the cooperative."

"The truth is that you fear one another."

I beckoned to Ramazan to bring tea for the men. Asghar, who now was a member of the village council, got to his feet to help Ramazan. This was no ordinary tea that Ramazan and Asghar served the Rish e safed. In addition to the tea, hot and fragrant, there were dried watermelon seeds, shelled apricot pits, cookies and candies. I held the delicate tea glass in its silver holder between my hands. "Always you have been taught to distrust one another. When you were a child listening to the stories of your grandfather the stories warned you to build a wall against your neighbor. Is that not so?"

Musi, the brother of Mash'hadi Mokhtar, nodded his head. "Can the partridge trust the hawk?" he asked.

"We must trust each other," I said, and I was surprised to hear that my voice was breaking with emotion. "The clinic, the bath, the school for girls, the sanitation of our village—all these are the fruits of trust."

The Kadkhoda got slowly to his feet. "We should form the co-op."

Mash'hadi Mokhtar leaned over to put his glass on the floor before him. "I and my brothers favor forming the co-op." Then he gave me a long searching look and I saw the flame of the kerosene lantern reflected in the depths of his eyes. "You are thinking of more than improved orchards and gardens, Lady Najafi."

"Yes, I am thinking of these things, but more than that I am thinking of the great dream of my life."

The next morning I rose early and walked toward the mountains. This I had always done when I was in need of solitude and strength. Already some of the village women were at the jube drawing their daily water. These I spoke to and their quick smiles and friendly eyes gave me courage. For all through the night I had been asking myself, "What if the hawk should eat the partridge?" I, alone, have urged the council to go against deep-seated caution.

After a time I had left the last cottage behind and around me the uncultivated hills lifted their round, barren shoulders. "This is the place," I said aloud.

For a long time—perhaps since I had first come to Sarbandan—I had been longing and half planning to build a factory that would give the women of Sarbandan an opportunity to add to their family income. I can't pinpoint the moment of my first dream nor do I know when the dream changed into a plan. When I had made part of my first village home into a workroom for women and had installed small looms there I had thought, *But a factory should never be built in the middle of the village as this workroom is.* When Shapoor and I had built our home on the edge of the village facing fields that stretched away to the mountains at the west I had thought, *Perhaps someday a factory should be built where this field is open and ready.* But that thought had given way to, *The people would think the factory was always under my eye, that it was my factory.*

But now I knew where the factory should be and the dream, the plan, had crystallized into a decision to act. "This is the place," I said aloud. "This is the place for a factory."

I sat down with my feet folded under me. Right here we should build a factory. It would not be a great operation. Perhaps sixteen or twenty looms, a few sewing machines, equipment for dyeing and stretching materials. Here we would not turn out the silks of Damascus or of Thailand, but cottons and woolens needed in Iran —and perhaps some special things for export, but these we would think of later. The women at the looms would be the very same village women that I had greeted as I followed the course of the jube toward the rising hills. If we planned carefully and divided the work opportunities, perhaps fifty or sixty women, working in three shifts, could spend some time in the factory, and thus increase the welfare of the village. The girls, too, could learn to use the looms and the sewing machines. They would not need to leave the safety of their villages and crowd into Teheran to find employment, or if they went to the city they could go as skilled workers with positions already open to them.

With the cooperative registered there would, perhaps, be an opportunity to borrow money for the factory. I had heard, too, that the American organization CARE was interested in establishing trade schools and small industries so that people could learn to help themselves. And yet I knew from all of my work in the village, especially from my experience with the building of the clinic for which the people themselves gave the land and the labor, that if my dream was really to materialize the people must share not only the dream but the effort that it takes to bring a dream to fruition.

I went back to my home for a morning tea and to say good morning to Mother, to Sina and to little Nassim. Then I walked to the teahouse. Mash'hadi Mokhtar met me, tea glasses in his hands.

"Mashdi Mokhtar," I said abruptly, "do you remember the first time that I stopped at this teahouse?"

"The best thing that ever happened to Sarbandan," he said.

"Perhaps." I shrugged since it is polite to shrug when one receives a compliment. "But do you remember that we spoke of the long winters?"

"I remember that we spoke of many things." The gold teeth

flashed under his preposterous mustache.

"Today I am serious," I said. "Will you come for a walk with me?"

"First drink the tea, Lady Najafi."

So we stood together drinking the tea, and his eyes searched for meaning in mine. "You are the man who knows all things in Sarbandan," I said. It was his turn to shrug.

Together we walked through the village and into the rounded hills. "Who owns this land?" I asked him.

"Many owners. It is grazing land. Perhaps it is owned by six or seven hundred people."

"We must have a meeting," I said.

Mash'hadi Mokhtar sighed. "So many meetings."

The next meeting of the Rish e safed was in the afternoon. Again we talked of the things that the village had accomplished. Slowly and carefully I presented the dream of a factory, reminding them that their wives had already learned to make carpets and ja-jims and gelims in the small workroom that adjoined the school for girls. And, after they had shared my vision of the factory with its busy looms, I waited for the inevitable question, "Who will give us this factory?" It came in several voices.

"Sarbandan does not wait for gifts," the Kadkhoda said staunchly, then he turned to me. "Already you know where this factory will come from."

"No, I do not," I admitted. "Perhaps the government, the Development Bongha, perhaps American CARE, perhaps—but who knows? This only I am sure of. You yourselves must make the start. If you give the land then we can say, 'See, the people of Sarbandan are eager for this factory. Already they have given the land. They wait to give labor and cooperation.' In this way the battle is half won."

"How much land?" several asked.

I took a deep breath. "Sixteen thousand meters."

"Sixteen thousand meters of land cannot be given in a day," another old man said, wiping his sleeve across his sun-peeled nose.

I looked at the men, most of them in clothes so patched that the original suit could not be told from the patches. Many of them were barefooted. To them I must look wealthy, indeed. "I do not ask for myself," I said. "From the factory I will get nothing. But soon I must return to Baluchistan and before I go I would like to talk to the government, perhaps to CARE."

Nassim wakened and cried, and although I knew that my mother would take her up and care for her I left the room and went to my baby. These men must decide for themselves whether or not my dream could be their dream.

They talked together. Sometimes I heard an angry voice, sometimes a persuasive one. Abruptly the men left. It was not until Mohsen had come for us and we were ready to leave that the Kadkhoda came to me.

"The land should be surveyed," he said. That was all.

"When I reach Teheran I will send a surveyor," I answered, keeping my voice as even as his. But my heart was leaping.

Back in Teheran I had no time to sit in my mother's house and visit politely with guests. I had little time to be a mother to Sina and Nassim. I had to see many people on business for Sarbandan. I had to find out for these men so willing to trust me and move ahead at my suggestion just how to organize and register the cooperative. I had to learn enough about the cooperatives to be certain that the people of Sarbandan were ready. I had to send a surveyor to check the land that the men were willing to give for a factory site.

There was just part of a short summer to do all of these things. Soon I would return to Baluchistan.

It was not hard to send a surveyor to measure the land for the factory I dreamed of. But it was with the men of Sarbandan as I had feared. When I was not with them, drinking tea and eating sweets and telling them of the value of cooperation, they were fearful. They were not ready to register the cooperative and without that we could do little. PLAN agreed to send two men to the village to teach special things about the cooperative and to prepare it for registration.

In Iran not the Shah nor the parliament, but a specially appointed committee of experts called PLAN Organization makes recommendations on how the national income, especially the profits from our fabulous oil fields, shall be spent. PLAN's first interest is to encourage agriculture by assisting the farmers to make better use of their resources and market their products more successfully. That's why PLAN was interested in the organization and registration of Sarbandan's cooperative. Working closely with PLAN are all the departments of government. It is the Development Bongha that is most active in carrying government help to the villages. The Development Bongha would send a dehyar, a man well versed in agricultural work, who could help the farmers to select new growing stock, new seed, who could demonstrate the use of insecticides and plant food. So many hours I sat in the offices of PLAN and the Development Bongha! So many men I talked to regarding this assistance to the village!

I went with Mr. Nadaff, the dehyar, to Sarbandan. Again the council met in my home. Again Ramazan and Asghar served tea and sweets and the dried seeds of watermelon. "Mr. Nadaff is a friend of the village," I told the men, who looked at me from under drawn brows. "You can trust him as you trust me."

He began his work very well. He let the men ask him questions, which he answered quietly and intelligently. "Dear God," I prayed to myself, "let him not push. Let him discuss with these men what must be done so that they will feel the idea is their own. Please, let him not push."

So many times I visited the village and stayed for days at a time that I said to the doctor's wife, "Who is it that lives in this house and who is the guest?"

She smiled and kissed my cheek. "You are always welcome. To me you are the heart of this village."

5 ❦ A Bridge Over Which to Walk

ABRUPTLY IT WAS SEPTEMBER. THE SKY WAS STILL A VIVID BLUE
and the sunlight was golden and alive. But the poplar leaves in
Sarbandan had changed to gold coins that turned and danced on
the trees and finally sifted through the air—no longer coins, but
now tiny sails adrift on the buoyant air. It was time to return to
Baluchistan.

During the summer while I had waited in government offices to
discuss with PLAN or the Development Bongha the problems of
Sarbandan I had carried a small sketch pad in my handbag. Working
a few minutes at a time I had designed a sheath dress which could
be decorated with Baluchistan embroidery from neck to hem. With
this might go a stole, embroidered in the same traditional pattern.
The dress should be black so the reds and greens of the embroidery
would show to best advantage. Perhaps both the dress and the stole
should be made from hand-loomed material to give them weight
and body. I had seen in Athens the beautiful clothing sold through
the Queen's Charities. I had thought of interesting our Queen in
such a project; or if not the Queen one of the Shah's sisters, who are
always interested in the welfare of the people.

Now that it was nearly time to return to Baluchistan I hurried to
purchase material for dresses, stoles, handbags, tray covers. Almost
before I had finished buying the meters of cloth, the thread, the
needles, Dr. Birjandi's office called to say that it was time to take
the two-engined plane to Baluchistan. Pooran came to stay with me
the night before our departure.

"Shall I take Nassim and Sina to the airport to see you leave?"

58

Fahkri asked as the family sat in Mohsen's house eating a farewell dinner. "Sina loves the planes."

I did not have an immediate answer. I had been consciously turning my mind away from the thought of leaving my babies but now I had to face the separation. All summer, in Teheran, but especially in Sarbandan, they had been close to me. Sina was now talking like an adult, commenting on everything around him, and Nassim was growing from a baby to a person.

"Let them stay in their beds in the morning. I will tell them good-bye tonight."

"They are already asleep," Mohsen's gentle wife protested.

"Still I will say good-bye before I go to bed."

Mohsen drove Pooran and me to the airport. I knew that Shapoor's family, and most of my own brothers and sisters, felt that I wanted to neglect my children, that I rationalized when I argued that I must support myself and the children at least as long as Shapoor was in school in America and that Mother would give them as good care as I could give them. They had even asked me if Sarbandan and Baluchistan were more important to me than my family. Pooran in the back seat was quiet and Mohsen said, "You should have been born a man, Najmeh. No one would expect a man to give up his work, especially a work that so few are prepared to do."

"Thank you, Brother," was all that I could say.

At the airport there was great excitement. Pahvine and Zahra were waiting to meet us and in a moment we were surrounded by the specialists of the Baluchistan Mission. Everywhere there was talk of Baluchistan and its problems. I said little. I hoped to surprise everyone with the success of our plan.

As we circled over Bampoor we noticed that the nomads had already returned; the tent villages seemed to sleep on the dun-colored plain. Almost before we were out of the plane the woman Effat came toward us. "We have been waiting for you, Lady Najafi," she said. "We are ready."

Suddenly I realized that I had neglected to do during the summer one important thing I had promised myself to do—improve my Baluchi. I had hoped that I could find an instructor in Teheran, or failing that I would spend some time every day reviewing my own vocabulary. The first day as we unpacked the goods I had brought from Teheran I suggested that we speak to each other only in Baluchi. As we worked more closely with the women it would be necessary that we communicate with them in a more precise way. We must all make a special effort. Only Zahra, who could not long stay with one thing, was in and out. She told us that the women were not in their tents, but were often talking with each other and some had even come hesitantly toward our government compound.

The next day we, the girls and I, went to invite the women to come to our schoolroom. During the summer those who had embroidered for us had told the others of the miraculous twenty-five cents a day. We now had our schoolroom almost filled with women who pushed each other forward and giggled and laughed among themselves with evident nervousness.

First, everyone must wash her hands. Water had been brought in empty kerosene cans and heated for this purpose. Scrub, scrub, scrub, and the collected dirt from many summers and winters rolled away, leaving the brown hands several shades lighter. The women admired their hands and compared them with Pooran's slender white ones. They were interested in Zahra's nails. No woman in Baluchistan had ever seen an emery board, a nail file, or even manicuring scissors. Nails, when they grew long enough to break, were chewed off to finger level.

It took several days to explain what we were going to do with the material. I drew a picture of the dress I had designed, and of the stole. I showed them how we planned to use the embroidery. No one needed to tell them about the embroidery. This they had known always. Even the young girls—some, barely out of their childhood, had come with the women—knew well how to use the needle and how to follow the traditional designs.

After the work was really begun we no longer needed to pay attention to the sewing. That could go on almost automatically while we talked of many other things. Sanitation, sanitation, sanitation. They must learn how to be clean before they could learn anything else. They were interested in grooming and we taught them to wash their hair, which they had always rubbed with oil until it was stiff and unhealthy. They wanted to care for their nails and we gave them the fundamental materials. They wanted to rid their own hair and the hair of the children of nits and lice. We taught them how to use a comb dipped in kerosene, and we advised them to cut the hair of the children if the kerosene treatment was too painful or tedious. And we furnished the scissors.

CARE provided us with fifty sewing machines, and we selected the most apt women to learn to use them to make finished items. Those who were most skillful were allowed to work on a traditional wedding coat. For this coat I had bought all of the material and was, myself, paying for the labor, since the coat was to be a gift to America.

Each day we were busy with the teaching while brown hands moved with dexterity and purpose over the material I had bought in Teheran. For the first time the women were really open to us. They listened, they learned. We learned. The girls had noticed that the children in the tribe were ruled entirely by fear. Even grown men and women found their lives controlled by the violence of their fathers. In America when I was a student there I had lived with an American family where the only rule was the rule of love. I had seen a six-year-old child take part in a family council and give advice to her parents which they considered with care. Later, on my second trip to America, I had seen this same child, grown in wisdom and self-confidence and ready to be a leader among her peers. In America I had learned that a man who in his childhood is governed by fear ordinarily will be either a brutal or a fearful man. As we sat together in the sewing room I tried to give this idea to mothers who, of course, were not prepared to understand it at all. The best way to reach them was through stories and in my simple Baluchi I often told these that I had heard as a child. I was astonished at how many of the folk tales of my country were horror stories—how hard it was to find stories of love and understanding to tell to these eager-faced women who sat before me. And so I told not only the Persian stories, but stories of other people and other lands.

And they in turn tried to give us the wisdom of their tribe in the proverbs of the people. These proverbs do not translate well, as the words in which they are told often have a double meaning. Here are some of them.

The goat which has the mange drinks from the beginning of the fountain. (He who should have the least wants the best.)

When there is a free mullah, even the kitten prays.

Be a lion in your own village rather than a coyote in the next city.

The old wall is held up by a buttress, but an old man is supported by his stomach.

When there is no father you must call the stepfather "daddy." (When you don't have that which you really want you can make do with something less.)

Between us—me, Pahvine, Zahra and Pooran and the women of Baluchistan—there grew a warm cooperative feeling. "God, I thank you that you have given us this bridge over which to walk into each other's hearts," I said whenever I prayed.

Working in the woman's program was not like building a road or a dam or an agricultural college. It wasn't even like building an irrigation system or planting a garden. The heart of a woman cannot be plumbed and measured.

Sometimes it seemed to us that the work crawled; but as we saw the finished pieces of embroidery pile up in our supply room we realized that this was one way in which we could check our progress, for every woman who had worked on the embroidery had come under the sound of our voice.

One day Pooran came to me with tears sparkling in her eyes. The women—some of them—had been interested in a book she had shown them, astonished that she could read. They had asked to be taught. We had planned to place the literacy program last, but since the demand was here the instructions should be available. I began with charts to put the reading on the basis of the lives of the women.

"I would be beautiful if all over I could be of this sweet whiteness," a young woman said as she scrubbed her hands before she began her sewing.

"That is not impossible," I said. And that day I told the story of the bath. I told of the old baths of Persia, where one could spend all day dipping in and out of the pool, eating cucumbers, and listening to music. I told them how mothers of sons looked over the young women who came to the bath to pick out a bride for the sons. Then I told them of the new baths of Iran. Here women may sit naked in the steam and scrub themselves and children, then go into the shower and come out all of a "sweet whiteness."

This to them was like a fairy story. But when Pahvine and Pooran and Zahra also said that this was so, even in some of the villages as well as in the cities, the women asked, "When do we get a bath?"

"This *is* not impossible," I said. "Much has already been accomplished. This, too, can come to us."

One Friday—for the women spent Friday with their families—the girls and I decided to check over the work we had done. We pressed and counted and folded. More than a hundred finished pieces. The women were ready for our literacy program. They were asking for a bath.

When we went to dinner there was a dark look on the face of Mr. Akhev, the head of our mission. He came and stood before me with his eyes looking at the floor. "Lady Najafi," he said. "As soon as possible you and the girls must kiss the Koran."

"No," I said, not believing what I had heard. Because in Iran to "kiss the Koran" means to go. What he was saying was that we were to leave Baluchistan. "I did not plan it this way," he said slowly. "But the woman's program has been discontinued."

"Who has decided this terrible thing? What does Dr. Birjandi say to the termination of this program?"

He still did not raise his eyes to mine. "Someone high in government has decided that the woman's program is of little value."

I knew that the government was in financial difficulty but the Baluchistan woman's project was so inexpensive! One hundred fifty dollars a month for my salary and one hundred for each of the girls. CARE had given sewing machines, needles, scissors and first-aid materials. The government budget had allowed only $1,300 for materials and the small incentive salaries of the women. What could saving such a small amount as this do to balance the national budget?

I left the dining room and went to my own room. I lay on my bed and watched the square of blue sky framed by the window. What of the hundred beautiful pieces we had pressed and folded—the pieces that were to mean the beginning of a new economic life for these women? No doubt they would go into some storeroom or perhaps even be given to people who could buy every luxury and might not appreciate the beauty of the handwork. But more important than the products of the women's hands were the women themselves. All that I and the girls and the women of Baluchistan had done to bring them out of the primitive time would be obliterated, just as a footprint is obliterated by wind-borne sand. For this unfinished, lost work I had been away from my babies for six months. For this unappreciated project I had delayed for half a year the work I needed to do in Sarbandan. I was crying, and I did not know whether the tears were tears of sorrow, or disappointment, or rage.

There was nothing to do but to return defeated to Teheran. In Mohsen's home I sought comfort with my children. But something had happened to my buoyancy, my ability to find something good in every situation. All I could think of was that my government had failed me. And not only me but the women who were open to me and my girls and who were willing to change their way of life. The government—or some important person in the government—could not see that each woman who had changed herself through work and study would rear a different family, with different attitudes and goals and aspirations; that to educate the mothers is to educate the hearts of the children.

Hearing that Dr. Birjandi was in his office I called on him.

"I know, Najmeh," he said before I had spoken of my disappointment. "We speak of *The Government* as if it were one person who can undertake a plan and finish it. No government in a democratic situation is like that. One group is in power and launches a program. That group loses the confidence of the people and another group with entirely different goals comes into power. That is one of the hazards of the democratic system."

"You mean that in our country everything is built on sand?"

"We are working toward stability." He moved forward on his chair and leaned toward me. "I am soon to be given a different post. You see what I mean. I cannot make long-term plans with any assurance of completing them."

"Dr. Birjandi, if I had an independent income I wouldn't work for the government. Instead I'd—"

He smiled as he interrupted me. "One of the engineers who observed you at Baluchistan spoke well of you. He said, 'Najmeh is the best field worker in the world.' "

"I am a field worker; but where is my field?"

Dr. Birjandi stood up. The interview was over. He had given me new understanding, perhaps new discouragement.

My family was careful not to add to my disappointment. Fahkri's husband said, "There is much work to be done. Anyway it is almost summer and the Baluchistan program must be stopped in the summer."

Fahti, not knowing much about the things she spoke of, said, "No learning is lost. Village workers can carry on most of the program with these women if the women have really been awakened."

But one cousin who had always been especially dear to me said, "Maybe you are through with this whole thing now. Maybe you are ready to be just a lady."

No Ruz, 1960, and I had never been so unhappy. Sina, two and a half, was old enough to watch his grandmother start the sabzeh, old enough to talk of gifts, of bonfires, of dinner guests; but I could not enter into the plans with any enthusiasm. Instead I stayed close to my own rooms. Nassim was learning to walk. I coaxed her to come to me from where I stood her against chair or sofa. She could almost get up from the floor without help from a convenient hand or piece of furniture, and when she fell down, her legs straight out in front of her, her little face registered surprise instead of fear, anger or dismay. I thought she was saying a few words, and I tried to put meaning to her constant babbling. Oh, she was charming and I should have been a happy mother, but I felt so useless. So betrayed, somehow.

As soon as No Ruz was over I put a few things in my suitcase.

"Sarbandan?" Mother asked.

"Sarbandan. Of course."

"Shall we take the children with us?"

"This time the children should stay home, Mother, with you. I will have much business to do. Besides I am so tired."

Mother kissed me and her soft face against mine was a blessing.

Mohsen drove me to Sarbandan. "When shall I come for you?" he asked when he let me out at the teahouse.

"I'll come back on the bus," I told him. "But first I must find myself."

I went into the teahouse and soon Mash'hadi Mokhtar joined me. His brother brought tea glasses on a shining tray and we sat facing each other on the narrow carpet.

"I am glad you are back," he said, smiling.

"And how are things in Sarbandan?"

"Good, very good, for this moment. The rice crop was good in Mazandaran and our young men returned with money." He waved his hand in a wide gesture. With my eyes I saw only the walls of the teahouse, but with my imagination I saw the early blossoming orchards. "There are many blossoms."

"And the crumbling house behind this new plaster?"

"Still crumbling," he said.

"Tonight I will meet with the Rish e safed."

That evening we sat in a circle on the floor of the room that Shapoor and I had built for just such meetings. Shapoor! If Shapoor had returned with me from America perhaps things would have been different. But we had agreed that he should stay. Now, sitting in this smoke-filled room and thinking of him beside me, I couldn't even really see his face. The image was there, but it was inexact, not clear.

The sharp eyes of the village men watched me from under heavy brows. Their look was both curious and trusting—a look long familiar to me.

"Well," I said, waiting.

"Sixteen hundred meters is much land," said one, coming directly to the point of the meeting.

"It belongs to many."

And the Kadkhoda said, "We will give it for the factory."

"You must vote so every one speaks for or against this thing," I told them. So they voted, every voice speaking out for a factory.

I had resolved to ask CARE, an organization that promoted self-help projects, to cooperate in the building of the factory. But before I could make this request I had to be able to show the officials of the organization that the people of Sarbandan needed this factory, that they wanted it, and, even more important, that they would seize the opportunities a factory would bring, working eagerly toward improving the situation of the village.

Making my home once again with the doctor and his wife in my little house, I began a careful study of the village. I checked on the school, the clinic, the slaughterhouse, now built away from the jube, the house for the bathing of the dead. I watched the women care for their children, keep their homes, look after their chickens. I talked with many about their way of life, about their plans for the future, and then, sitting by a lantern in the evening, I drew up a careful report of all the villagers had done since they had awakened to the modern world. The next day I took the bus of Mash'hadi Mokhtar back to Teheran.

Sina ran to meet me as I got out of the taxi before my mother's home. "I have been lonely for you, Mama," he cried, wrapping his arms around my legs. "I cried for you."

I would have taken him into my arms but he would have none of it. "I was lonely for you, too, darling. But now I am back."

I took his cool, slim hand in mine, and noted that it was no longer the square little hand of a baby.

When I held out my arms for Nassim she turned away from me and grasped a handful of her grandmother's hair. "Ma-ma-ma-ma," she said, and Mother said, "Najmeh-jun, we think she is speaking."

I had thought that my children were like my mother; that I could leave them any time and when I returned they would be just as I had left them. Oh, a little older perhaps, but still a part of me and willing to accept me.

"CARE must wait," I told myself firmly, and I devoted myself to Sina and, when she would have something to do with me, to Nassim.

But the thought of Sarbandan was always with me and one day I telephoned CARE and made an appointment to see Mr. Sakalis, the head of the organization in Iran. He received me without seeming to patronize me as so many officials do any woman. He was gracious, courteous, thoughtful. First we talked of CARE and its distribution of American surplus food as salary to men who were working on valuable projects. The Sarbandan area needed roads. Some villages that look close to Sarbandan on the map are hours away by donkey trail. Perhaps roads could be built in our area which would bring the remote villages into our circle of education and sanitation. Later we talked about the village and about my experience with small industry. I told him of how the villagers themselves had built a clinic, enlarged the school, built a new bath, voted land for a factory. I told him of my training in America, where I had been a student for a time at the Los Angeles Trade and Technical College, which trains young men and women to take a place in the trades and in industry.

"We will give this consideration," he promised. "CARE still uses the CARE package as a sort of symbol of the help we want to give those in desperate need, but now we are much more interested in helping people to help themselves. We are not a self-perpetuating organization in any country. Our plan is to start some worthwhile projects, turn them over to nationals, and leave. Your plan for a factory may fit in with our plans. It very well might."

The interview was over. Mr. Sakalis had made no promise; he had named no time. He hadn't even arranged for another interview, but somehow I felt more hopeful than I had for many months.

6 ❦ Light for the Shahsavan

As I SAT ACROSS THE WIDE POLISHED DESK FROM MR. MALAK MAN-
soor my eyes went from the massive diamond on his finger to the
thoughtful brown eyes behind heavy glasses. He had sent for me
and I waited for him to finish the usual pleasantries and tell me why.

"Do you know Dashte Moghan?" he asked.

"In a general way."

"I have been given the responsibility of resettling the Shahsavan
tribes in that area." His fingers played a drum rhythm on his desk.
"I want a woman's program in Dashte Moghan. Are you the woman
to plan this program and get it started?"

The men of Sarbandan who had given land for the factory were
eager to get it started. Perhaps I shouldn't take a position so far from
my village.

Yet my work at Sarbandan was a "work of heart" and I could not
afford to be without regular employment. Besides Dashte Moghan
was garmsir, winter land, and I could do much on the Sarbandan
project before I would be needed in Dashte Moghan. Nothing could
be done on the factory in the winter, anyway, since most of the men
would be working in the rice fields of Mazandaran, where the
Caspian Sea made winter along its green shores as warm as a mountain summer. Even had the men been at home, little building can
be done where everything is snow-covered.

Accepting Mr. Mansoor's offer would not delay the factory at
Sarbandan—at least not much—and it would mean salary again
and peace of mind. I thought of Sina and Nassim.

"I would wish to take my children," I told Mr. Mansoor.

"Of course. Servants, too, if you wish. Several of our engineers will have families there. Your husband?"

"He will be in America for at least another year."

"I had hoped you would be available. Learn all you can about Dashte Moghan. I shall expect a firm answer soon. "A servant brought me a sheaf of papers and almost before I knew it I was standing on the sidewalk looking up at the blue sky through the almost naked branches of the white sycamores.

Dashte Moghan. Even the name had a romantic sound.

Dashte Moghan—the Plains of Moghan—has been important in the history of my country from the earliest days. Many think that the River Aras, that laid down so much of the sediment that has formed this plain, is the river mentioned in the Avesta and that Zoroaster, who might have been born in 1100 B.C. but who was certainly born before the time of Cyrus, grew to manhood near the shores of this river.

Since ancient times the plains have been a strategical battlefield. Long before the Moslems invaded Iran there were well-organized patrols there, and after the conquest the Islamic kings built mosques and schools and carvanserais. Ruins of some of these remain. Shah Abbas quartered his army there. Much more recently the plains were a battleground between Russia and Iran. Gradually, because of the weakness of the central government and because those in power did not care about Dashte Moghan, the fertile plain and the cities deteriorated and the once important plain became a wasteland. Now Mr. Malak Mansoor was appointed to make them once again a place of importance.

This much I knew of Dashte Moghan. This much everybody knows.

From the material Mr. Mansoor gave me to study I read that much had been happening in Dashte Moghan. In 1950 the government had decided upon settling that plain with the Shahsavan tribesmen. Accordng to the brochure, PLAN had tried both unirrigated and irrigated farming and had now completed two canal systems so that all of the land could be utilized for agriculture. The land had been opened to the tribesmen and they had eagerly applied for settlement and landownership. On each hectare of land stood a modern house and there were villages, public baths, clinics, schools. Each family could earn a yearly income of $1,125, ten times the average farm income of Iran.

To me Dashte Moghan sounded like Paradise.

I was ready with Mr. Mansoor's "firm" answer.

"I am glad you are interested," he said when I telephoned him. "Now what I want you to do is this. You go up to Dashte Moghan— at our expense, of course—and look over the situation for yourself. Then you can give us a report of what you think a woman's program could accomplish."

I have always been afraid of escalators. I would rather climb ten flights than to step onto these moving stairs. But in these days my heart was like an escalator. First up, then down again, then up again. Right now, thinking of Moghan, of Mr. Sakalis' promise to consider the factory, of the children much closer to me since my summer with them, of Shapoor with just one more year to spend in America, my heart was at the top. I sang to myself or to the children. I played with Sina and Nassim. I even called on friends, giving my whole heart to the pleasure of being alive. My entire body vibrated with a feeling of well-being.

I was concerned when I didn't hear at once from Mr. Mansoor about my trip to Moghan, then I was informed that I was to travel with him and two of his engineers, and since Dashte Moghan is garmsir, we must wait until the people would be down from the mountains. It was the middle of October before we set out.

The ride to the Moghan Plains, eleven hundred kilometers from Teheran, was a long, arduous one: one long day to the city of Resht on the Caspian Sea, another longer one to Dashte Moghan on the Russian border. But the trip was not tiresome. Malak Mansoor had a special respect for women, an interest in their education, in their projects. We showed each other our deepest feelings, our highest hopes. More important than all the money PLAN had decided to spend in the area were the mind and heart of this man who would be the director of the program.

It was night when we approached Alirezabad, where our headquarters was constructed. I saw lights upon lights, more than in the city of Tabriz. Really, seen from a distance, we might be approaching Shiraz or Isfahan.

"The lights," I cried, shivering with excitement. This would be different from Baluchistan. Here the people would be ready for the program.

"The lights," one of the young engineers repeated. "Wait."

So I waited until we stopped outside a dark village, the only lights a few flickering lanterns carried in the hands of young men. Our camp lay in darkness on one side of the river. A Russian town, blazing with electric lights, on the other. Fifteen miles between the Russian and Iranian settlements. Fifteen miles and perhaps a century.

After tea I was taken to my room. When I was ready for bed I pushed back the curtain from the window. The moon was just lifting and in its light I could see the plastered compound, and away some distance a huddle of whitewashed cottages. I got into bed, keeping my eyes on the sky and waiting for the moon to sail into the dark blue square framed by my window. I understood now why the government had made Mr. Malak Mansoor the director of the project. Our people, settled in Dashte Moghan, could always see the Russian countryside. They could see, for the first time perhaps, how life can be lived in a more advanced civilization. My government should make Dashte Moghan the most beautiful part of agricultural Iran so that there would not be this difference in the two sides of the river. My heart trembled with the challenge.

Next day we visited the cramped headquarters building. Four engineers shared one room. The doctor shared a room with most of his equipment and two engineers. Even the clinic was small—no larger than the one the villagers had built for themselves in Sarbandan.

The people were living in their tents but soon some would be moved to cottages built under the direction of French and Italian experts. I visited the cottages—single rooms with walls almost as thin as paper and with none of the niches Persians build in their cottages for the storage of bedding in the daytime, for sacks of grain, for clothing hung under bright ja-jims. In these houses there was a place for absolutely nothing and I thought if I were a nomad I would move back into my tent.

As we walked from place to place we saw a few women and children, who paid no attention to us. They had beautiful expressive eyes and sunburned faces, and they were dirty beyond belief. They even looked dirty to one accustomed to Baluchistan. And the river was so near! I stopped to speak to four little girls, each with a baby tied on her back, who were squatting in a ring. They looked up inquiringly, but their faces were without understanding. When they returned to talking to each other I recognized they were speaking Turkish. Another problem!

The agricultural program was already thriving. In spite of the winter-naked branches there was beauty in the seventy-hectare orchard and garden that had been planted partly to furnish fruit and vegetables, partly to produce the twenty thousand seedlings needed each year for replanting in the reforestation project, partly to show these nomadic people what could be done with patience and care and love.

Those were the ingredients of my work, too. Patience and care and love.

When I returned to Teheran I had much to do. There was always Sarbandan business to take care of and this time, since the children would go with me, I had more shopping to do, more packing. As I packed with one or both of the children always under my feet I was constantly reminded of packing to come home to Iran just two years before. Then I had had to think only of Sina and myself; now it seemed that Nassim's things and the clothing for the servants took more than half the space. I felt that I was always leaving something, somebody. I wondered where the two years since I had left Shapoor in America had gone; but looking at the children, Sina questioning anxiously if we would be gone forever and Nassim babbling, "Mama, plane, go, go," I knew that the years had certainly brought change and development, at least for the children.

Sarbandan, shopping, the packing, the children's care—these

were spare-time activities. My real work was to interview many applicants and choose the women who would assist me in the Dashte Moghan program.

Pooran and Pahvine I would take, of course, if they wished to go. In addition I chose Mehri, gentle, beautiful and blessed with initiative; Zorah, just out of high school, whom I promised, "I will hold you in my hand"; Homah, a childless widow who danced when she walked and whose face was radiant with life; and Mrs. Hosseini, older and as experienced as I, who had worked in the Varamin area and had studied a year in America. Mrs. Hosseini was Turkish and could be our interpreter, and Homah was a kindergarten expert.

In Sarbandan when I had not known how to begin my work, an epidemic of summer sickness had forced me to open a simple clinic. Mothers had brought their babies to me and had stayed to learn of sanitation, disease prevention, child care. In Dashte Moghan sick children would be cared for by the doctor and I would never see the mothers. We might reach the children through a kindergarten, the mothers through their children. I told something of this plan to Homah and she was enthusiastic.

I wrote an excited letter to Shapoor. This position, largely administrative, would be a challenge to me. The salary was good. I could have the children with me. I would take Ramazan and Nannie with me to take care of my quarters and look after the children. I would invite Mother to go, too, but she might be reluctant to go that far from Teheran. She had been having trouble with one of her legs, and though she never mentioned it I had noticed that when she prayed this leg did not bend with the other and when we sat on the carpet with tea glasses in our hands this one leg was always thrust out in front of her.

Before we were ready to leave, Shapoor's mother came to call. I thought she had come to bid us farewell and I was pleased. She had come to ask me to leave Sina in her care when I went to Dashte Moghan. Shapoor had written that he didn't want his son reared by servants. What could I say? "Taking care of a small child can be very taxing," I told her. "You have reared one family, are you sure you wish to start on a second?"

"We have discussed it. We think it is best if you are willing."

"Give me time to think it over," I asked, but even as I spoke I knew that I would do what Shapoor wanted me to do. In every letter he spoke long and lovingly of his son; seldom did he mention the little daughter he had never seen.

It was January before we started for Dashte Moghan. New jeeps had been purchased by the government for the project and we traveled in these. What a crowd! My six girls, Zorah's grandmother, who felt she must chaperone her eighteen-year-old granddaughter; Nannie, Ramazan, Nassim and I, and with us twenty young graduates in agriculture from Karaj College. Shapoor's parents had come for Sina the night before. It was easier for him to leave me than to see me leave him.

For three days the jeeps pulled up the mountain roads. It was just beginning to get dark when the caravan was stopped for officers to check our police cards. Since we were going close to the Russian border and the Communist party is outlawed in Iran, we all had to have security clearance.

And now, abruptly, it was dark and from a distance the young people saw the unaccustomed glow of lights. They insisted on stopping the jeeps while they got out to jump up and down and shout their happiness. I did not say, "Those are Russian lights. We are they who will make the light for the Shahsavan."

When the jeeps drew up at the compound Mr. Malak Monsoor was waiting for us. Zorah tumbled out of the station wagon first and said, "Is this—it?" She had expressed the feelings of everyone.

Mr. Mansoor gestured toward the compound. "This is—it." And then he shepherded us into the dining room, where a cheerful round-faced man served us a sturdy tea.

"Your rooms are ready," Mr. Mansoor told us, and with pride he showed us the rooms he had had prepared for us. In each there was a carpet, an ancient radio, four chairs and a bed. We had all brought bedrolls so one bed in each room was sufficient.

Nassim and I slept in the bed; Ramazan and his aunt, Nassim's nannie, on the floor. I don't know how the girls arranged themselves but for a long time after we were quiet there were talk and laughter and more talk from the girls. I said nothing. The holiday would soon be over.

The next morning I rose early to ask Mr. Mansoor what the arrangement was for food.

"You may cook for yourselves because there is a market here and many foods are available. However, we have a kitchen and a cook. Each of the men gives the cook some money each week and he buys and prepares the food. This morning you and your girls are our guests." I had reached the door of his office before he called me back. "And if you have time look into the kitchen and see what goes on there. Ali, the cook, is a funny fellow and so proud of the little Farsi he knows."

"A woman's place is in the kitchen," I said with a laugh.

"I hope Ali thinks so." He laughed, too.

So the first person I knew in Dashte Moghan, outside of Malak Mansoor, was Ali.

Ali was a young man, perhaps between twenty and thirty, though he already had a wife and a mud house of his own a little outside the government compound. He was a noisy fellow, filled with life and tricks. From the first I learned that he put his nose in every door. There was nobody's business that he didn't take an interest in and the responsibility for discussing it with everyone else. I soon learned from the men who ate in Ali's dining room that they were paying enough to eat a banquet every day. What they were getting was far from a banquet. The kitchen should be my first responsibility.

One morning I found out how much money Ali had been given for a week. Then I went into the kitchen when he returned from the morning shopping. "How much is this for each kilogram?" I asked him, touching a leg of lamb.

Smiling broadly he gave me the cost.

"How much did you pay for the whole leg?"

Again smiling he named a sum.

I took a scale I had borrowed from Malak Mansoor's office. "How could that be? Someone cheated you, Ali. You paid for two more kilograms than you received."

Each item I considered in the same way. Ali never lost his smile. Finally, "I now see that there is no one honest in the whole market," he said.

"Especially dishonest is Ali," I told him. "Tomorrow you should put oil in your body." In Iran it is thought if there is enough oil in the body a whipping will not be painful, and so this is a playful threat to punish.

"Yes, Lady Najafi," he said with a disconcerting, impish grin.

The engineers had begun to worry that if the food kept getting poorer and the servings smaller they would soon get no food at all. But now the food began to be much better for the money and the men were pleased.

"There is too much work to be done with all of these great eaters," Ali insisted, so I sent Nannie into the kitchen. Here she laughed so much and ate so much that she gained twenty pounds and one day fell on the floor from overeating. She was demoted back to the care of Nassim.

Next we hired a helper named Mahmood. This doubled our trouble and once Pahvine lost all of her savings. How did these boys put their hands on it? No one knows. When Ali was accused of stealing he said blandly, "Do you think I am a Turkoman?"

"I *thought* you were Shahsavan," I said. But he only smiled and made me laugh with a droll remark.

These dishonest clowns could not be replaced because they had been employed by others so could not be dismissed by me alone. Besides, who would I get in Dashte Moghan that would be so cute, so funny, so good-natured, so willing to work from six in the morning until after nine at night, so incapable of complaining or saying, "I'm tired"?

Mr. Mansoor had asked me to find out what happened in the kitchen. I reported on the dishonesty of the cooks, on the clouds of flies that must be exterminated, and I gave enough guidance to improve the food. After some time we even employed a woman to prepare the vegetables in order to leave Ali only the shopping and fancy cooking. After all, I told myself, Ali is not the only man in Iran who uses his position to make some side money; and Iran is not the only nation where this is a practice with many.

Except for planning the menus and making sure that there were fruits and vegetables even out of season, I left the kitchen to others. There was so much more important work to be done.

I began my work as I had in Sarbandan and Baluchistan. I walked through each of the villages quietly and carefully, taking notes on what I saw. Sometimes one of the women, or some of the younger girls, would stop to talk with me. Mrs. Hosseini I had always with me to interpret for me. The girls began their observation in the same way. At the end of the first week we met together in my room, sitting around a lighted lantern on the floor, our feet drawn under us in the Persian way. Together we made our plans. The agricultural program was almost ten years old. There was a clinic with a capable young Parsi doctor, there was one school for the children of government employees but no other opportunity for education.

And so we decided that we would begin with a kindergarten, first in Alirezabad under the direction of Homah, who knew kindergarten work; later each of the girls, having learned from Homah, would go to a separate village.

There was no building to house a kindergarten so we asked for a tent. The children came to our beautiful red tent because they were curious. It was Homah who turned that curiosity into interest. She understood not a word of Turkish and they understood not a word of Farsi, but she sang to them, taught them to play a circle game, showed them toys that could be admired and enjoyed but not played with—yet—and had them listen to the soft music of wind chimes. The other girls watching Homah were open-mouthed with wonder and admiration. I was, too, but my eyes left the radiant Homah to rest on the dirty little children with the rings of white nits around their hairlines. Kindergarten and singing were good, but these children must be clean. When I mentioned this to the doctor and to Malak Mansoor they agreed that cleanliness was a fine thing, but they left me to discover how to obtain it.

Since there was no bathhouse in the entire area I had to devise my own equipment. I started with a large oil drum, which was placed in a hole in the sand so only a few inches lifted above the level of the earth around it. In this way there would be no tipping of the barrel when the children jumped around. Water was brought from the river, heated over an outdoor fire and poured, warm, into the clean oil drum. Then a child was lowered into the drum. Mrs. Hosseini, speaking in Turkish, soothed them while they soaked. Accumulated dirt of even a short lifetime does not come off in a moment. And while they soaked we cut off most of their snarled, knotted, matted hair and deloused the little that we left. As soon as a child was clean we dressed him in the cheap cotton uniforms I had purchased in Teheran and sent him to the doctor.

Those were busy days for our young doctor. He found trachoma, tuberculosis, many functional diseases, even leprosy, in our flock.

After each bath the water was siphoned out of the barrel and fresh water and another child put in. This was a slow project and the work was backbreaking. We had thought the mothers might gather around us but instead they stayed in their tents or huddled in the background in disapproving silence. Of course all of the children could not be bathed in one day—the operation took several days. In fact, Pahvine, blowing the hair out of her eyes and locking her hands across her aching back, said, "There aren't as many children in all of Teheran as we have put through this bath."

By the time that all the children under eight had been taken through the process, the chairs for the kindergarten had been delivered. Now the older people did gather around to see the chairs. "How can I send my child to sit on a chair?" mothers asked. "After a while what will they ask of us?"

The wind blows most of the time over Dashte Moghan and it constantly carried sand into the tents. After the spring rains came, the water ran into the tents too. But Homah didn't mind sand and water. She began her program with nearly a hundred children and soon divided the group so she had an afternoon and a morning session. It was amazing how fast the children learned Farsi. They sang Farsi songs, of course, and there were always things to be counted in the new language: children who had combed their hair, children who wanted a cookie or a glass of milk. Long before I could converse with anyone in Turkish these little ones were chattering away in Farsi or listening with unbroken attention while Homah or I told a story.

My days were long. At five each morning I wakened, prayed in the Shi'at Islam way, lighted the samovar, then wakened Nassim if she wasn't already babbling to me. I bathed her, dressed her, fed her breakfast. I could always hear in my memory Shapoor's mother saying, "It is not well for children to be reared by servants." And at these times when Nassim was so close to me I missed Sina with an almost physical longing. Nassim was walking wherever she wanted to go, so as soon as she had finished breakfast she went to waken the girls, crawling over them in their beds and wakening them with a kiss. Who wouldn't want to be wakened by that sweet elfin child?

Whenever I chanced to look out of my window, even if the time was not yet six o'clock, I saw the children waiting outside the kindergarten tent although the class did not begin until eight. They sat or stood quietly waiting until Homah opened the tent flap. Each in turn shook hands with Homah, "Salaam, I am Hoscin," "Salaam, I am Malmood," "Salaam, I am Effat." After this morning greeting each child washed his face and combed his hair because our facilities were better than those in the home tents. They went to the latrine at the kindergarten, too, for at home there was no such facility. The day's program began with singing and one day I sat down beside a little boy who sang loudly all on one note. First I sang a tone, then I waited for him to sing it. He sang, out of pitch and without music. I tried again and again.

"It is always so, Lady Najafi," Homah said. "I think he doesn't hear."

That afternoon I took him to the doctor. The child had a low percentage of hearing; he heard only a loud noise close to his ear. This was the first case of deafness we had noted. The doctor examined the ears. "Maybe if I could clean some of this wax out of the ear I could see what I am doing." I watched while he removed the hardened wax and dirt. Carefully he put oil in the ear from time to time to soften the wax. At last the ears were clear. The doctor put his glass on his eye. "Now I shall see," he said.

"What do you see?" the child asked.

The doctor and I looked at each other, neither of us ashamed of the tears in our eyes.

"We must do this for each of the children, Dr. Mazda," I finally said over the choke in my throat. "I think that there are no others who have lost their hearing because of this wax, but perhaps there are others who do not hear well."

"One doctor," the young Parsi said, and he spread his hands at the futility of trying an extended program with such limited personnel and facilities.

Only Homah could do the work of many. For the first time in their lives the children were eating with plate and cup. CARE supplied milk with cookies or bread for a mid-morning lunch. She insisted on perfect manners and the children complied.

One day she came to me. "There are three children who cry all the day. What shall I do?"

"Why do they come to the kindergarten if they are not happy?" I asked.

"Perhaps they were sent by their mothers, their aunts, their cousins."

"Why do they cry?"

"For their mothers."

"Let them go to their mothers."

"How then will they learn?"

"Homah-jun, many people find it hard to see the things they have to give refused by those who need them most. The children will miss so much—but so do the adults when they cry after the old customs and traditions."

The children loved excursions: to the big cooperative market, to the great garden where the seedlings for reforestation are grown, to the river. They walked two by two, singing as they went, and people stopped in the street to see them go by. They had never owned a toy in their lives, so one day I brought in two American hula hoops.

The children lined up and took turns and some got so proficient they could have twisted from morning until night without dropping the hoops.

One day we had a visitor from Teheran, Mr. Afkhami. He visited Homah's kindergarten and watched the children at their singing games. "These children are having their first taste of happiness in a child-centered world."

"After this experience will the children revert?" I asked.

"Some, perhaps, if there are too many pressures on them. But most? No. Once a man has learned to be a human being he never again wants to be an animal."

By the first of March each of the girls was located in a separate village. Each had carried out a bathing and delousing project, each village had been visited by the doctor, and in each there was a kinder-garten. I prepared for each of the girls a mimeographed form for a village survey. What is the population? How many have been born this month? Register these new babies with their names and the names of both parents. How many have died? Register these names with approximate age and cause of death if known. What is the condition of the drinking water? How many will stay in Dashte Moghan during the summer?

I worked long hours in the office, work that I do not enjoy, and after the girls left I was lonely. There was Homah, of course, and Pooran was not far away. It was Nassim who was the center of my life.

But now it was March and soon it would be No Ruz. I had looked forward to Shapoor's being home for the holiday but he wrote that he wanted to see a little bit of the world on his way home. Well, if he didn't see America and Europe now he might never see them. Sina would be as disappointed as I. How hungry my heart was for Sina.

7   ✤   No Ruz

"Najmeh-jun," my sister Fahkri said when she met me at the airport, "you are tired, tired, tired."

I hadn't known that I was tired until I was seated in the plane as it circled above Dashte Moghan. Once again, as I looked down upon the Russian sector and compared it with the Persian side of the border, I realized there was so much to do, so much to do in every way. On the ground, the kindergarten of Homah, the beginning work of the other girls, the irrigation and drainage canals, the huddle of new cottages, all looked impressive. In the air they seemed just a small start. And so I was tired.

"You must forget work for a month. No Sarbandan, no business calls, no shopping for Dashte Moghan."

Fahkri could forget these things because she is exactly woman, concerned with her beautiful home, with making comfort for her husband. I said nothing because already I had planned to do much during my short stay in Teheran.

At Mohsen's house my mother held the Koran for me to walk under. And there was a surprise. Mohsen had called at the home of my husband's family and brought Sina. I had wondered if he would be weaned away from me, but now he wrapped both arms around my neck and said, "Mama-jun, I cried for you. Every day I wanted to see your face." The uneasy feeling that I might have made the wrong choice shook me as I held him close, his soft cheek against mine. "My face is getting wet," he said. "Don't cry, Mama."

"What do you want to do first?" my sister Fahkri asked. She had come to greet me, her arms loaded with carnations.

"First I must arrange for Nannie and Ramazan to go to Sarbandan to their families," I said, "and then I must go to the bathhouse."

The family laughed. In the home of my sisters and Mohsen and my mother there is, of course, a bath. But why should one miss the beautiful steam, the pleasant massage, the company, of the bathhouse? "I will go with you," Mother offered and so, with Sina and Nassim, we went to the bathhouse.

There is no luxury like being clean down to the bottom of every pore. To go into the steaming room, to relax and give oneself to the hands of a gentle woman, to talk with Mother, to have my children, two perfect cream-colored little bodies, climbing over me and cuddling against me—this is perfect happiness, pleasures unknown to those accustomed to a quick shower or a lonely soak in one's own bathtub.

For a month preparations had been going on in all of the homes of my family: housecleaning, painting, gardening, sewing, shopping, cooking. And when we returned from the bath my mother, with Sina jumping around like a frisky puppy dog, brought out the sabzeh. The sabzeh is a plate of wheat or barley seeds that germinate in water. Already each green shoot was about three inches tall. Mother had tied a pink ribbon around the growing grain to make it specially festive. It is an old tradition that as these grains germinate and grow they absorb all of the tensions, the troubles, the unhappiness of the family in the home. "We do not need a sabzeh; there is no unhappiness here," I told her, but she knew from the shine in my eyes that I was happy to follow every tradition.

"We will even have bonfires in the courtyard. That's my secret," Sina said. I grabbed him up and kissed him. It seemed that in the few months I had been away he had changed from a baby to a little boy with all of the words that he needed for grown-up conversation.

The Wednesday before No Ruz, Mohsen's boy brought the faggots for the three small bonfires, and as soon as it was dark the fires were lighted in the courtyard. It is traditional to jump over these fires—every member of the family should jump—and as we jump we say a verse which does not translate into a verse at all.

"*My yellowness* [*sickness*] *to you,*
Your redness [*health*] *to me.*"

For the first time Sina thinks that he must jump over the fire. The bonfires are small, but he is even smaller. Mohsen and a cousin jump him high in the air so that the flames are many inches below him. And I wonder, will the progress I am working so hard to bring to Iran erase these beautiful traditions? But no, America has Santa Claus, and feasting at Thanksgiving, and sentimental cards at Valentine's Day. Traditions and progress are not incompatible.

After we had jumped over the fire we went into the dining room. There are certain foods to be eaten on this night; the most important is a dish made with fish and chopped vegetable and egg. These things have a special meaning.

The children were undressed and ready for bed when a knock came at the door. Sina, stumbling over the feet of his American sleepers, hurried to open it. There stood four little girls beating their little brass bowls with spoons.

In some parts of Iran women who have illnesses in their homes go from door to door beating a spoon upon a brass bowl. They have their chadars over their faces so no one knows them. The householders put into the bowl the ingredients to make a soup to cure the sick. Children imitate these women, but into their bowls go watermelon seeds, candies, cookies, all sorts of good things. Once when I was a child I went with friends, beating my spoon against my bowl. One woman took my hand. "This is the hand of a lady," she said, "smooth and slender and fine." Now as we filled the bowls with good things I looked at my hands. They were still slender, still smooth, but now they were the hands of one who worked. It had never been my method to give instructions and watch the work done; rather I had explained the process and worked side by side with the learner. I saw the little hands holding the bowls. Some had cracked nails, some were a little dark at the knuckles; but these were well-fed hands. I thought of the clawlike hands of the children of Baluchistan. One can't banish sorrow from one's mind by making a decision to do so. Sorrow comes like an uninvited guest to sit in the

The factory at Sarbandan, surrounded by the village-built retaining walls

The "knocked-down" machinery being set up at the factory

The weaving instructor
from Tabriz

Najmeh instructing at the loom

Najmeh with CARE officials and villagers (*U.S.I.S. Iran*)

Sarbandan's
most competent weaver
at work (*U.S.I.S. Iran*)

Gelim, a woven rug, sometimes used as a bedspread or blanket, from the looms of Sarbandan

The teahouse of Mash'hadi Mohktar (*R. E. Jones*)

A tent home in Dashte Moghan

The kindergarten in Dashte Moghan

Mrs. Hosseini's cooking class

The Health Clinic in Dashte Moghan

Houses built for the villagers

Nassim, Najmeh and Sina with the No Ruz Sabzeh. (In the tradition, the sprouting grai
germinated in water, absorbs the unhappiness of the household.)

mind even in the happiest hours.

With much laughter and romping I put Nassim and Sina to bed, then rejoined the family for the booming of the cannon that would announce the vernal equinox at the exact second. Here were all the members of my family who lived in Teheran. But Shapoor was still in America. If only Shapoor were here the circle would be complete.

Directly after the roar of the cannon Mother, in the traditional way, took the Koran out of the house and brought it in again. The Koran must come into the house before any guest in the New Year. This is a symbol of the place of God in the home. Many go to the mosque to pray when the cannon sounds; others, like my mother, find a quiet spot in the home.

And so it was No Ruz, a time for gift giving like Christmas in the West. For everyone there is some gift. First the servants must be remembered. In Iran we employ servants for small wages, but we are responsible for all of their needs—every piece of clothing, every pair of shoes, every haircut. No Ruz is a good time for giving a new suit and a pair of two-toned shoes to Ramazan, a dress of figured rayon and a new black chadar to Nannie. These they had taken in a package to Sarbandan. For Nassim and Sina and Mohsen's children there were toys, and for the grownups perhaps a piece of jewelry, some delicate soap, some perfume, a potted plant or cut flowers. All day long there will be guests and for each of these guests there should be a gift.

On the carpet in Mohsen's salon a beautiful banquet cloth was spread. On the cloth were seven foods beginning with S: vinegar, garlic, sumac, apple, jujube fruit, smoked fish and olives; a sweet pudding made of wheat, and the sabzeh. There must be a bowl of goldfish—not to be eaten—silver, a mirror, a jar of rosewater, a lamp, a Koran, a bowl of hard-boiled eggs, yogurt and cheese.

There will be many guests at dinner. In fact, some people go away for the holiday to escape so many visitors. Shiraz, Isfahan and the Caspian resort cities are always crowded.

For seven days the visiting in Mohsen's home continued. Always there were guests for every meal. The children were hysterical with the excitement of continued presents. Sina shocked us all by greeting cousins with "What did you bring for me?" At one family dinner party each person sitting cross-legged at the banquet cloth had someone kneeling behind him reaching over him for food. And everywhere there were laughter and happy talk.

On the eighth day after No Ruz the men always return to their work. Mohsen has a place of business both in the city and in the bazaar and it was time for him to buy and sell more carpets.

"Mama, where are you going?" Sina asked as he watched me put on my suit and high-heeled shoes. "Grandma, Mama is going again," he shouted as he ran to find my mother.

"Not for long this time, Sina-jun," my mother said.

"Not for long," I echoed. "I have an appointment to see Mr. Sakalis at CARE."

"Must you work when you are at home for just a day or two?" my sister-in-law, Mohsen's wife, asked.

"Yes," Mother answered for me. "Yes, Najmeh was always this way."

And so I saw Mr. Sakalis. CARE had been working on the Sarbandan project. The land survey had been completed, the titles checked. Everything in this complicated deal was in order. Mr. Sakalis said that he felt very hopeful. I had prayed for a firm promise, but since I had absolute confidence in Mr. Sakalis if he felt hopeful I would feel hopeful.

The thirteenth day after No Ruz is Sizdah-Bedar (thirteenth day out) and everybody including the Shah goes on a picnic. "We could have our picnic in the courtyard," I suggested. But Mohsen had planned a surprise for me. "Today we will take the ranch wagon." Mohsen had recently bought this American automobile, part car, part truck, and he was very proud of it. In the wide front seat there was room for the driver and two or three passengers. The open truck box could be neatly covered with its own sleek matching canvas or, open, it was exactly right for hauling small loads or large families. "We have planned to go to Sarbandan."

Taking the ranch wagon meant that part of the family would sit in the back on ja-jims, part in the cab. This informal arrangement would make the picnic even gayer. We didn't get started until mid-morning since there were so many preparations. Not only does each family take an enormous picnic hamper, but the samovar must go along, for what is a picnic without tea? Nowadays, too, like Americans, we must take a case of Pepsi or Canada Dry along for a taste treat. I insisted on sitting in the back but I was overruled. It seemed, sitting inside the cab with Mohsen and his wife and Mother, that all the fun was outside in the truck. We passed thousands of picnicking people. The poor who do not have bus fare spread their picnics on the sidewalks. Especially around a park or a square where there are grass and flowers, people love to sit on the sidewalk and look at the growing things. Persians never picnic on the grass. They know how hard it is for the grass to grow and they respect it.

People with a little money in the pocket take the bus to the end of the line and picnic anywhere there is an open spot. Some go by camel and many by foot.

In Sarbandan we picnicked in an open orchard. Barely had we taken the children's toys from the car and spread our blankets when the brother of Mash'hadi Mokhtar appeared. "Lady Najafi," he asked, "do you plan to come to the teahouse?"

My family groaned, but I said, "Yes. I have some news for the council and for your brother."

"He has some news for you," he said darkly; then went away whistling.

We all laughed and after a time I walked to the teahouse. Mash'hadi Mokhtar was waiting for me. "Will you come to my house?" I asked him. "And shall we call the Kadkhoda?"

He nodded and sent his brother running with the summons.

While the family picknicked under the blossoming trees I sat with several members of the village council on the front porch of my house, looking out over the greening field.

First I said, "It is well that you gave land for the factory. The survey is in order and so are the deeds. CARE is very hopeful."

"When will we have the factory?" two impatient men asked almost together.

I lifted my shoulders in a careful shrug. "Who knows? These things move slowly."

"Lady Najafi, did you know that we no longer have our perfect doctor?" Mash'hadi Mokhtar asked.

"I have seen him in Teheran. He and his wife came to call on me. He is very happy at the university," I said. In Iran a doctor who has completed his premedical work may take charge of a clinic like ours. He comes to us with only book knowledge. He hasn't had any internship, has had few laboratory courses. But a young man who loves the practice of medicine and has a feeling for the people he treats can do very well with this limited education. Of course, from the first he plans to leave as soon as he has saved enough money to do his advanced work.

Our doctor had been especially good. He had understood the people he took care of. He had been so neat and clean that they had learned cleanliness from him. His wife, too, was not only competent but gracious and charming to everyone. Oh, we had been fortunate in the couple who had been sent to take charge of the clinic. This had been especially important since Mash'hadi Mokhtar had given the land for the clinic and all of the men of the village had given labor. Sarbandan had been able to turn over to the Department of Health a clinic all ready to use. There were a waiting room, an examination room, a treatment room and a supply room. Sarbandan had been so proud of the clinic.

"Surely the Department of Health has sent another doctor," I said.

Mash'hadi Mokhtar spoke. "We have a new doctor. He is not good."

"Any doctor would be a disappointment after the excellent doctor we had," I said, "but we shall grow accustomed to him."

"Not this one," they all said, pouring out their anger. The new doctor had not rented a house to live in as our first doctor had rented mine. He had moved his entire family into the clinic, occupying every room, including the treatment room. What was worse, he had a wife, a mother-in-law or mother, and nine or ten children and all but one were girls! Some claimed there were eleven, not ten. No one kept the place clean. The mother thought the way to toilet train the children was to let them run around in shirts only, living like animals, and the clinic smelled so much that no one would go near it. "It is better to die of disease than to smell this odor," the tall Kadkhoda said, and all of the men agreed.

"What must I do?" I asked.

"You must visit the clinic and speak to the doctor."

"It is better to die of disease than to smell this odor," I said, but no one laughed. This clinic belonged to them. They had built it with their own hands and they each felt personal ownership.

"And then you must visit the Department of Health and tell them to send us a new doctor."

"I will write for you and you will sign your names," I suggested. "This is your clinic."

"We will try this but it will not work. Surely you know someone who knows someone who . . ."

These men knew how things are done in Iran. It is good to know someone. "First I will write for you. Later I will visit the department if it is necessary."

"And will you see the doctor?"

"It is not my business. But, yes, I will see the doctor."

Mash'hadi Mokhtar smiled. "The clinic has a hole in the wall. The winter made the hole. We will not repair it until a new doctor comes or this doctor becomes clean."

"But if you do not repair it," I said, "it will grow larger and soon the entire clinic will disintegrate."

"What good is a clinic without a clean doctor? What good is a clinic that is like the filthy home for the sheep? What good is a clinic that—"

With a hand I silenced him. "I will do what I can," I promised.

On the way back to the picnic I passed the clinic. The men had been right. The stench of stale urine, of human excrement, met my nostrils as I went by. Several children were playing on the doorstep. And there was the hole in the outside wall that no one could mend until there was a good doctor.

Abruptly Sizdah-Bedar was ruined for me. For the first time I realized that even in Sarbandan progress is not self-perpetuating. Anything that I had built through the hearts and hands of the people I loved could be wiped away by one slothful person, just as the clinic was now useless. "God," I prayed, "help me to keep my heart up."

"Najmeh, what is the matter?" Mother asked as soon as I rejoined my family.

"Everything will be right when I have eaten some delicious country bread." I gestured toward a new-baked loaf.

"Ramazan's mother sent the bread," Nannie said proudly. "My sister is the best for bread baking."

I would not let my dark spirits ruin the picnic. With determination I lifted my eyes to the blossoms on the trees above us. Soon these blossoms would change to fruit. This year the fruit would be harvested and sold to the wholesale market in Teheran so there would not be any waste, any surplus product. And after the sale would come the payment of last year's debts, the lessening of fear for a few months at least, the celebrating of marriages. No Ruz was surely the time for new hopes and dreams, not for worry about a deteriorating clinic.

Nassim, tired of toddling about over uneven ground, began to cry, I took her into my arms and soothed her.

"I am a newborn flower from the garden," I sang.

> "In the dawn I awaken with the murmur of the zephyr
> And the murmur tells me that in this beautiful day
> You are to welcome a very dear thing. . . ."

After Nassim had dropped off to sleep and we had made her comfortable on a blanket, we walked down to the jube and Sina threw the sabzeh into the running water. With it went all of the misfortunes, the old quarrels, the unhappiness of the past that it had absorbed as it grew from seeds to fresh green sprouts. But there was no sabzeh that had absorbed the worries about the clinic and all of the other worries that I could do nothing about. There was nothing that I could throw into the stream as I began a new year.

8 ❧ The Flood

IT IS SPRING IN DASHTE MOGHAN. AS IN ALL OF IRAN WHERE THERE are orchards of peach, apricot and cherry, the blossoms spread a fantastic veil of beauty over the orchards of the Department of Agriculture. But, if there had been no blossoms, spring would still have been evident in Dashte Moghan. In any garmsir, winter grazing land, the first evidence of spring is the stirring of the tribes, the preparation for the move to the grasslands in the high valleys for the summer.

When I returned to Dashte Moghan after the celebration of No Ruz in Teheran I felt this stirring as something electric in the air. The sheep were being sheared. From this place the wool could reach the markets more readily than from the mountains, if the sheep carried it there on their backs. The women were busy with preparation of food and packing of clothing and bedding. Only the boys and girls in the kindergarten were unchanged; they gathered at six o'clock and waited until eight when Homah opened the tent; when they saw Homah they ran to wash their hands and smooth their hair; they clapped their hands and sang and counted and chanted their Farsi verses as if tomorrow weren't going to be their last day in this enchanting place.

Of the sixty-five thousand people in Alirezabad and the villages around it only five thousand would stay on the plains during the summer. Our program would be exceedingly successful if we could persuade ten thousand to stay the next summer.

Of course all sixty thousand do not leave on the same day; all do not take the same route. The animals must graze as the tribe moves so the nomads leave tribe by tribe, each choosing its own route.

Each night before a tribe's departure the women dress in their finest clothing. There are dancing and singing and those who are not leaving participate with the tribe that is being specially honored. The morning that a tribe leaves the whole camp is astir before sun-up. The women, wearing their best clothes, kneel on the sand, their foreheads to the earth in the Moslem manner. On these occasions we government workers keep out of sight. Watching the women pray, my heart and prayers are with them. After the prayer all those who are leaving find their places in the line as if they have been rehearsed for this moment. Actually the same trip has been taken so many times that there is no question of where each man, each child, each animal shall go. Since tents are the nomad's shelter wherever he stops, the tent poles are carried with them. One pole is fastened at each side of a pack animal. Often a load of folded tents, of bedding or of clothing is bound to these poles and dragged in a manner of travel that was used by all primitive people before the invention of the wheel. There will be little rest along the way. They will come down only for lunch and dinner, but they have learned to jeer at fatigue.

With the few who chose to remain in the village and cooperate in the government resettlement program we were urged to intensify our efforts so that perhaps another five thousand would decide to remain the next year. We had reached the children. If the choice to go or stay had been left to them no one would have moved to the mountains. But we hadn't reached the parents. The girls and I decided to begin to work on the program in a strictly woman's way. We would give a tea in each of the kindergartens and invite the mothers to attend. The government workers scoffed at us. "Where do you think you are? In Teheran, perhaps? Or in Shiraz or Tabriz?" They predicted that no one would come and that all of our preparations would be wasted. But the men were wrong. More than a hundred and fifty mothers came to at least one of the teas.

The first of these teas was held in the large red kindergarten tent in Alirezabad. Each child brought his mother to the door. "Salaam, Homah, I am Hosein and this is my mother." Then, "Salaam, Lady

Najafi, I am Hosein and this is my mother." The children, accustomed to the kindergarten, were much more poised and sure of themselves than their mothers. When the children withdrew there was an awkward silence before neighbors began to chat together.

On a long low table we had my silver samovar singing with hot water for tea. There were trays of cookies and sweets, some of which we had made ourselves, some of which had been imported. We also had fresh fruit, brought quickly from Teheran.

In any ordinary school tea there would have been samples of the children's work decorating the wall. One of my sorrows with the kindergartens was that we had been unable to preserve the imaginative pictures that the children had drawn, their first Farsi writing. We had not had paper and crayons and pencils and their work had been done on washable slates, even in the sand. We did have the charts from which the children learned to read and to count and these were a matter of great interest to all of the mothers. One mother said to me in halting Farsi, "See, I speak. My boy has taught me." Another asked, "Is there any time a kindergarten for mothers? We must also learn to count and to read."

Mrs. Hosseini spoke to the mothers, who sat quietly and listened to her fluent Turkish. It was unlike their dialect of that language but they could understand all she said about what we were trying to do for their children.

It was evident that the children had instructed their mothers on manners acceptable to Homah. The mothers, most of them, ate as we had taught the children to eat.

In the mothers' tea in Number 2 village a woman who spoke passable Farsi said to Pooran, "I am Zahra. I speak to thank you."

"Why do you thank me?" Pooran asked.

"Yesterday when I was kneading the dough and waiting for the oven to warm up, Akram, who is five, and Ali, who is four, came and stood near the oven. They both waved their hands with all their strength. I became very angry. 'What is this new game?' I asked them. 'Have you learned this bad way of acting at the kindergarten?' Then they explained, 'If we do not wave our hand the flies will sit on the dough, and Pooran has shown us that flies carry germs that will make us sick. We do not want to go to the doctor for the injection.' "

Zahra lifted her hands and smiled. "I am thanking you for this. I am thanking you for teaching my children to live a long life and be healthy."

The teas were more successful than we had dared to hope. Besides they showed us that our instructions of the children had already reached the mothers and the kindergartens had been more than training for the children. Women, like Zahra, began to ask for classes for themselves. These were the requests we had been waiting for. Quickly we organized afternoon classes for mothers in each of the villages.

At first Mrs. Hosseini was the principal teacher but soon, sooner than we had expected, the mothers began to learn Farsi as the children had done. Besides the Persian language we taught counting, the alphabet, reading from a *Near East Reader;* but our greatest interest was to teach these women to be human beings. We taught culture through sanitation, grooming, manners. As in Baluchistan much of this teaching was showing, not explaining, and even the mothers who were slow to learn Farsi watched with eager eyes.

As soon as all of the classes were running smoothly I began meeting with mullahs and heads of tribes to discuss programs. It is never easy for a woman to meet with men, especially men of importance to themselves and their followers. It was unusually difficult for me since I had to depend upon an interpreter to talk with most of these people. How I longed to speak Turkish. I resolved to learn just as soon as I had moments by myself. But for now I must be myself, handling the discussion so that the men would present the ideas I had in mind.

A community that depends for leadership upon government employees, upon any strangers, cannot progress. There is an old proverb that a boy who lives within his father's tent all his life can never be as great as his father. The tribesmen must stand, as they have always stood, alone. But if they are to move toward a better life there must be a difference in the way they stand, in the things they stand for. For this change it is necessary to have active community councils, elected community leaders. Many times when we found ourselves behind a wall of prejudice and superstition, almost unable to move forward, we looked with longing across the Russian border to where a dictator could force a forward movement; but always we regained our courage and were content to move more slowly. Holding an election to name village leaders sounds simple to people who have been reared in a democratic situation. But the tribes have always been ruled autocratically by the khans, and before we could hold an election in Dashte Moghan we met the men time after time to prepare them to take part in a democratic election. Although now the women may vote in Iran, at that time there was manhood suffrage only, so my work was with the men. Pooran carried on the women's program with seldom a stumble.

Still I kept my finger on the pulse of the entire program—the kindergartens, the women's classes, the special classes for men and boys.

While we were so busy with the program I was grateful for Dr. Mazda and his efficient clinic, but one time he was badly burned and Pooran and I had to take over the routine work. There were other times, too, when I was called into medical service.

One day Pooran came hurrying in. "Lady Najafi, come quickly. Naheet will be dead if her baby is not delivered." I remembered Naheet, a beautiful girl who attended our classes.

I pushed back the papers I was working on at my desk. "I will come," I said.

I followed Pooran through the village. Outside the mud hut a clutch of men sat smoking and now and then speaking some word in a monotone. Other men knelt apart, their foreheads to the ground, praying. Some had climbed to the roofs but I could not tell whether they were praying to Allah or the mysterious animal born in their deep superstitions and called *All*. No one has ever seen All, this creature that preys upon pregnant women, but still they believe it comes quietly into the hut and, opening the abdomen of the waiting mother, removes the intestines. They believe that before a birth every approach to the house must be guarded or closed off to keep the creature out.

The jube must run past the house to carry away all evil spirits.

Even then All may enter and so a stick is put over the top of the mother's bed and an onion is placed on the top of the stick to frighten him. Even after the child is born the mother should not be left alone because All might find her and take out her lungs. A relative of the new mother should kill a chicken and hang it on the top of the well; or if there is no well some barley should be put in the bed with the mother. A horse is brought into the room. If the horse smells the barley and goes toward it the mother will live.

As I followed Pooran to the hut of Naheet I thought about these superstitions and how they might have risen from the things that go wrong at an abnormal birth or because of uncleanliness and infection. I wondered what superstition was standing in the way of Naheet's delivery.

I pushed back the curtain that covered the one door to the hut. Inside the dark room the smoke was like a heavy blanket shutting out the fresh air. All around the room women were sitting, smoking on their pipes. Like the men they were speaking only sometimes. All of the religious objects that could be borrowed in the village were hung in this one room. I do not believe that religion is superstition, but sometimes the two are braided so tightly together that not even an eye familiar with both can separate the strands. Two girls were walking Naheet between them. She cried out in fright and pain and the great drops of perspiration rolled from her cotton-white face. Over her head she wore the white scarf of her marriage day. The bridal scarf is always worn at the time of birth with the Shahsavans.

Normally birth is not so difficult among these people who live close to nature. A large tray is filled with ashes and over the ashes a towel is spread. On each side of the tray there is a brick for the feet of the mother. The mother puts her feet on these bricks and squats close to the tray. In front of the tray a kinswoman or a friend sits. The mother steadies herself in the squat position by locking her hands behind the neck of this woman. Sometimes another friend massages the lower back. The midwife sits behind the tray and delivers the baby. The water and blood are absorbed by the ashes in the tray; the baby is born onto the towel. When the birth is accomplished the mother may rest on her pallet for a few hours, or, like an animal, she may go on at once with the things that are needful in the care of the child.

But this was different. The child could not be born.

"Do not cry," I said soothingly, and my voice told her what my Farsi words could not. "I must help you if I can."

A quick examination told me that unless the child was taken Caesarean it could never be born and the beautiful seventeen-year-old bride of nine months would be lost.

I sent Pooran hurrying for Mrs. Hosseini, who happened to be in Alirezabad for a meeting. It seemed almost an hour before she returned, though I knew only a few minutes had passed. Through Mrs. Hosseini I spoke to the young husband, who waited, drawn-faced, outside the door. "How long?"

"Three days." This boy couldn't have been more than seventeen though he had a luxurious beard that would have been a fabulous decoration for a man of forty. His eyes were pain-filled, but his mouth was sullen. "I sent to the doctor for medicine. He would send no medicine."

"Medicine cannot help. We must take your wife to the doctor."

"No."

"I will take her. I will watch over her and be with her all of the time."

"No."

Perhaps if I angered this boy he would allow us to try to save his wife.

"You want her to die so you can marry another," I taunted him.

Suddenly his eyes filled with tears. "She cannot die. She is mine," he said.

"But she will die. There is a way to bring this child. We can put your wife into a deep sleep. Then with a knife we will make an opening in the belly and lift out the child. We will then close the opening and soon your wife will again be well."

"And who does this with the knife to save the life of my wife?"

"The young doctor," I said. "Dr. Mazda."

"She must die, then," he said. "She must not be dishonored."

Here was tradition stronger than a young man's desire for a living son—stronger than his love for his wife.

"Lady Najafi, you can do this thing with the knife."

I looked into the grief-distorted face of the boy—from inside the hut I heard Naheet, whose cries had turned to an animal-like mewing. A lie would save the life. I alone could make the decision. "God, shall I lie?" my heart said; then I smiled at the boy. "This I will do," I promised.

And so Pooran and I and Mrs. Hosseini and all of the women who had been sitting in the tent followed the young woman to the clinic, carried in her young husband's arms. "You must wait outside," I told the women through the mouth of Mrs. Hosseini. The women turned to prayer. We three took her into the clinic. Hesitantly I gave the shot that would close her eyes to the sight of the doctor, her ears to the sound of his voice. Then Dr. Mazda came in by the window. I scrubbed to assist him.

The child was a boy with a cry loud enough to be heard by the women outside the door. Two of the women tied a handkerchief to the end of a stick and signaled the news to the men who were praying beside the hut and on the rooftops. The mother of the girl, standing near the door of the clinic, put her forehead on the earth and prayed; then she took a handful of dirt and showered it through her fingers as the Moslems do at a burial. "God, I thank thee that this, my daughter, is returned to us."

In an hour Naheet had recovered from the anesthetic and was dressed in clean clothing. Four men carried her on a pallet to her hut. Around them the women danced and sang. I followed, carrying the child. I wanted to show him to the father. "You have a fine son," I told him. The young man, who had been sorrowful, afraid, angry, hopeful, adamant, again hopeful, was now too full of joy to speak. Finally he said, with tears running down his face, "May God keep you as he has kept my wife." In the hut I put the baby at the feet of his mother. This way he could have warmth, the feeling of nearness, without the danger of contamination.

The Mullah called the whole town to a prayer of rejoicing and for six days the family, close and distant relatives which meant most of the people, celebrated this birth—and the third day was the happiest of all. On this day the barber circumcised the child. The baby was dressed in a long white dress, as is the custom. There was the music of drums, a puppet show, dancing and singing. After the noisy celebration everyone went to the mosque.

The girls and I enjoyed this celebration (though we were not a part of it) because it could so well have been a funeral. I told all of my girls about the lie. In the life of the tribes there are vigor and gaiety, grace and vitality; but there are also stubbornness and devotion to outgrown customs, useless taboos. Never must any of us speak of the doctor's entering through the window or the people would lose confidence in the entire government program. But can one tell only the truth while a young mother dies?

Sometimes we felt that we were making real progress. Then we found ourselves singing when we rose in the morning, and our frequent meetings together were festive, happy hours. But sometimes we felt that everything we had accomplished was ephemeral and perhaps useless. We wondered if the plans for the future would ever work out. "The whole trouble," I told the girls one night as we sat about in my room discussing our problems, "is with the people."

"Especially the men," Pahvine said.

Sometimes we felt that the walls of superstition were crumbling but at other times that we hadn't dislodged a single stone.

When progress on our program was especially slow I often lay on my bed looking into the night sky and thought of Sina in the home of his grandmother. "Perhaps his grandmother will teach Sina that you are not a good mother," one of my cousins had written. If she taught Sina this, she would teach only what was in her own heart. She like other women of her class feels that a mother should not leave her home and family to take other responsibilities. And, there alone with only Nassim to comfort me, I often wondered if she wasn't right.

I had also had fleeting suggestions in letters from Teheran and

America that Shapoor's friends and relatives were telling him that I was not a good wife for him. Mother and wife, myself, a worker for my people. When Shapoor returned home and we could make our life together I would show him what a wife I could be!

It is autumn on the Plains of Moghan. Each day new nomadic groups return. Each evening there are tents where in the morning there had been no tents. So quietly do these people come that if it were not for the evening songs and dancing they would make no ripple on the smooth surface of life.

One day one of the leaders of the tribe came into my room. I invited him to sit down and have tea with me, but he remained standing and kept his hat on. He didn't speak my language and I couldn't understand his, but finally he let me know that somebody or something waited outside for me. When I followed him out he pointed to his wife seated on a horse. Without dismounting from her horse she proudly showed me that she was wearing twenty-six petticoats under her voluminous skirt. I smiled in appreciation, though at that time I didn't know that honor is measured by the number of petticoats!

That she had come to honor me told us all that our program was acceptable to the men who controlled the tribes. It was even appreciated.

As the tribes returned we watched and listened to see how much of the work of the summer would be carried to the returning nomads by those who remained with us.

We understood from the women that the summer in the high mountain valleys is more pleasant than the winter on the plains. They told us that many marriages take place in the free greenness of the summer grazing lands. And yet we noticed with pleasure that volleyball, a game that we had introduced after many of the groups had left, was as popular with the returning youth as it was with the young people who had played all summer. We noticed that the people who had just slipped back onto the plains were as enthusiastic about the daylong picnics with their planned sports program as those who had participated all summer. It was as I had thought.

Anything that we taught these people about settled life they in turn would teach to others. Teaching is a continuous chain; starting with one the learning spreads by contact and almost by magic.

When a forty-one-gun salute announced the birth of a Crown Prince our villages went wild with rejoicing. In any family in Iran a son is much more to be desired than a daughter, but in a royal family a daughter is almost no use at all. The birth of the little Crown Prince sent my thoughts back to the days in Pasadena when Sina had just been born and I could hear Shapoor saying, "My son is the most beautiful baby in all of the nursery. My son has curly hair. My son . . ." From Sina I heard very little. Each time my family wrote to me they told me that he was well. No one had time to tell me about the new things he was saying, the different things he was doing. And from Shapoor . . . Now, instead of letters about our friends in Pasadena, our household, his cards came from the cities he was visiting. The cards did nothing to bring him closer to me. But soon . . .

On the plains everyone settled down to the work of the winter. Land must be plowed, clods broken, seeds put in the soil. Winter clothing must be made. More than a thousand meters of material came from Teheran for the women to make into shirts, trousers, skirts, petticoats, scarves. In the classes the women bent over unfamiliar knitting needles in silent concentration, working on jackets and coats. The women were learning to wash the wool sheared from the sheep and the "lost wool" the children had painstakingly gathered from the bushes the sheep had rubbed against in passing; and how to card it by rubbing one homemade carding comb against the other.

By December the homes that were being built in the permanent villages were ready for occupancy. There were homes in villages 1, 2, and 3. In villages 4, 5, 6, the people would build their own homes with some help from the government. Already in these areas the men had begun to throw together shelters of cane or to dig caves.

With two of the engineers I visited the houses of villages 1, 2 and 3. I had visited them before when only a few were completed. Even then I had felt that they were inadequate. Now that I knew the women who would be trying to keep house in them I found them even less desirable.

"Where can you put anything in this house?" I protested. But the men laughed. "To people who have lived their lives in a mud hut or in a tent this will be a palace."

"A tent has more room than this, more air," I told them. "When will men learn to let women design the houses?" The men laughed again. "There is not even a place in this house for the smoke to escape, except by the door."

"The khorsee makes little smoke," they said, "and they will cook outside."

"But there is no courtyard."

They shrugged. They were thinking that I was hard to please.

A visit to villages 4, 5, and 6 left me even more troubled. These flimsy cane structures would never stand through the winter. A heavy rain—and Dashte Moghan does have rains—would flood the caves.

"The people should not be allowed to move into these structures until they have all been approved," I said.

"Lady Najafi, do you think you are in America?"

This I heard very often when I was discontented with haphazard planning or building.

All during December and January we worked in our women's classes to teach the women to keep permanent homes. When people move from place to place they can leave their dirt behind them. In permanent homes everything must be kept clean and sanitary.

Before the actual move began we held a meeting: the engineers, the heads of each program and I. I had determined to keep as quiet as possible at this meeting because my dissatisfaction with the housing had been discussed all over headquarters. But of course I was unable to. The plan, already drawn up, was to move all those who were to occupy the new villages at one time. Every family, scheduled for resettlement, would leave the old villages within a day or two of each other.

"But what chaos that will cause," I protested.

"How would you do it, Lady Najafi?"

"I have learned to move slowly, slowly. I would send a few families to each of these villages—not more than five or six. I would get these families settled and I would watch them to discover what problems they face, what difficulties they have in adjusting to this new way of life. When their problems are solved I would send close relatives—brothers or sisters—to settle next to them. Those who had met their own problems could help the newcomers to adjust more rapidly. In villages 4, 5, and 6 the later families to move could live with the first settlers as guests while they completed their own houses."

"That would take all winter," the eager young men protested.

"Perhaps."

"But the Shah is coming to inspect Dashte Moghan. Before he comes everyone must be moved."

I had said what I had to say and I was silent.

In February the move was made, all of the people at once as the men had thought best. And it was chaotic. People who had unhesitatingly found their place in the line to cross the mountains to the upper grasslands had no guides for this move. But move they must and take all of their possessions and animals with them. Seeing the unsheltered animals, the household stuff piled in haphazard heaps against the outside of the white walls of the houses of villages 1, 2, and 3 at the doors of the hastily thrown up shelters and the mouths of the shallow caves, I prayed, not entirely to God, "Please let there be no rain for a time at least."

I wakened one morning after a restless, dream-filled night. At about midnight I had risen and stood with my curtains pulled aside to look up at the quiet and distant sky. There had been stars, sharp and white in its blueness. Later I had gone to the window again. The dawn had not come but the stars had disappeared. And now as I rose for my morning prayer it seemed to me that the blue of the sky had been replaced by a peculiar yellow-gray covering that was tucked under the earth on every side. After I had completed my prayers I went outside my room and watched the first large drops of rain splash into the sand and leave little indentations but no moisture. As I turned to go back to my room I heard the low growl of thunder in the distance.

I wakened Pooran. "The animals are still unsheltered in villages 4, 5, and 6," I told her. "These poor people have almost everything they own still outside their homes."

Pooran always wakened with a sunny face. This morning the smiled disappeared. "What can we do?"

We had barely got to Pooran's door when the scattered raindrops ceased to fall for just a moment. It was as if some giant had caught them in his hand, then the moment passed and the water came in a sheet as if the rain were a river pouring over a precipice.

"A cloudburst," Pooran said.

We stood close together in the doorway, the falling water like an impenetrable wall before us.

"I think I knew that this was going to happen," I said. "I'm sure I knew." I tied a scarf over my head. I must get to the dining room. Perhaps the engineers would already be at breakfast. "My poor people," I said, just as my mother would have said the same words.

In the dining room we heard that two of the young engineers had left in a jeep to see what could be done. "Surely this rain can't last long," each person was reassuring someone else.

Abruptly the door was thrown open and the engineers seemed to leap into the room. "The canal has given way. Villages 4, 5, and 6 are in the path of the moving wall of water and we can't get to them."

I closed my eyes and saw this wall of water pushing into the caves, trapping anyone who had sought shelter from the heavy storm.

"Come, there must be something we can do."

We piled into the jeeps, but we couldn't get near the flooded villages. The thunder of the water almost covered the terrified bawling of drowning animals. On the breast of the water, animals, household goods, sleazy shelters gyrated wildly. Never in my life had I felt so strongly the cruel unselective arm of nature sweeping over the puny possessions of man.

Since the jeeps could not get through we turned back. "The people have saved themselves," one of the engineers told me.

"How do you know that?"

"Did you see any human bodies in the flood? Animals, yes, but not people."

If the people had saved themselves they would be helpless without tents, blankets, food. Hastily we called a meeting and sat together.

"What shall we do first?" the engineers asked each other.

I was ready with an answer. "The first thing we need is water."

There was a burst of laughter, though everyone knew that a lack of pure water would bring an epidemic more fearful than the flood. In Parsabad there was an excellent well drilled by the French. This we could count on to furnish the water we needed, but it would have to be carried to the flooded area and distributed to the people. I wondered if these men who had been so eager to move everybody at one time now felt uneasy with the knowledge that what might have been a minor incident was now a major catastrophe. The people who had been stripped of everything they had worked a lifetime to gain would blame the government. And why shouldn't they? It did no good to tell ourselves that no one can predict a cloudburst, a flash flood.

After the wall of water had roared by and the rain had stopped, we again climbed into the jeeps. The need for food and water would be immediate. Even the four-wheel drive of the jeeps could not combat the deep sticky mud that covered the plain, the water still standing several inches deep in dimples all over the surface. Well, if the jeeps couldn't function, a tractor could take us. But the tractors were almost as helpless as the jeeps in the grasping brown sponge. Yet the people must have help. Many of us set out on foot. I was especially concerned about Pahvine, who was working in the new villages, but my heart cried out for the helpless villagers. We soon discovered that the mud sucked at our shoes and stockings so we discarded them and went barefoot.

Someone thought of the sure-footed donkey, who, if he is willing, can get through anything. These, as many as were available in the old villages, we loaded with basic supplies.

When we reached the main course of the flood, everywhere in the mud were the bodies of dead chickens and animals; some of the animals were almost completely covered with the flood's sediment with only a leg or an ear or a nose sticking out. Behind the bodies of larger animals debris had piled up and made weird semi-shelters for the dead beasts. Already the bodies were giving off the sick dark smell of death. Soon we would have to form burial squads to put these animals under deeper earth. But now our mission was to the living.

In village number 4 we found Pahvine. Engineers from Parsabad had got through with a tractor and a tanker of water. Pahvine was distributing this water one cup at a time, remaining sweet and quiet even when the frenzied villagers were insistent on a larger share.

And now we found that the information that the settlers had escaped the flood was not accurate. Many had been caught in their caves and drowned, helpless to escape through the swirling, incoming waters. The dead must be decently buried. When an animal dies the problem is to dispose of the carcass before it contaminates the area around it. When a man dies the problem is not one of disposal but one of dignified, reverent preparation of the body for its long rest until judgment day. This Islam believes. And in time of chaos, especially, the higher sentiments, love and affection and reverence that exist in the family, must be nurtured in order that man may rise above despair.

"There must be water for the washing of the dead," I said.

In all of the disaster, from the time we watched the wall of water sweeping over the plain through our attempts to reach the villages, I had remained calm and businesslike. But now as I saw the villagers giving their ration of drinking water for the washing of the dead, the tears came into my eyes and I turned away. There would soon be more water from the great well in Parsabad.

And so, before the cleaning up, the digging out, had really begun the funeral processions moved slowly and with solemnity toward a cemetery that would be built in a day. It was as if a shroud had wrapped the poeple. Some of them dragged themselves aimlessly back and forth through the mud. Some sat in the mud to their waists and prayed. I could see that if their lives were to be saved they must be wakened from the shock which had conquered them completely.

Water must be brought from Parsabad, food from Alirezabad, hope for the future from somewhere, and I had not yet found where. The canal water would have to be diverted from the broken channel so that the wall could be mended, but this would be the work of the engineers. The people must somehow be motivated to dig themselves out. Perhaps tents could be borrowed from those who lived in other shelters in the old villages and in villages 1, 2, and 3 not touched by the flood. All of this I would leave to the engineers. My work would be directly with the people.

But when, exhausted, we gathered again at our center in Alirezabad, I was told bluntly that the engineers would rebuild the canal—but that was all that they would do. Most of the trained manpower and all of the equipment would be needed to build an airstrip at Parsabad so that the Shah's plane could land there. The Shah was coming in three days. Had I forgotten?

Our Shah is a compassionate man. Had he been in Dashte Moghan at the time of the flood he would have been the first to hurry to the stricken villages even if he had had to go as we did, on bare feet. But the engineers thought only of the formality of the occasion. There must be the airstrip even if the people . . .

Pahvine and I took charge of the distribution of food and water. The young girls could not help with this. But most important in this work was a good mullah, and Allah gave him strength. He was everywhere, comforting the people, encouraging them to do what they could for themselves, bringing them together in a mosque which had miraculously escaped the flood, helping them to find comfort and hope in prayer.

Everywhere the people were told, "Ask Lady Najafi. She will help you."

And in my heart I was saying over and over again, "God be my help."

9 ✤ The Visit

FROM THE MOMENT THAT THE WALL OF WATER HAD SWEPT OVER the broken bank of the canal I had forgotten that the Shah was to pay us an official visit and that I and my girls were to bring our four hundred and eighty kindergarten children to be reviewed. When the chief engineer told me that all of the heavy equipment and most of the men who were working in the flood area would have to be taken to Parsabad to build an airstrip for the Shah's plane to land, I wondered how I could have forgotten the enormous task that we were expected to perform. This is the sort of project that is usually thought up by men for women to do.

First the children had been taught how to behave in formal circumstances. Our little ones, sternly and sometimes cruelly disciplined at home, had learned some measure of self-discipline in the kindergarten. We had worked day after day to teach them to be courteous and thoughtful of others. I had often smiled to see the children imitate the quiet sweet ways of their teachers. At the same time we had made an effort to teach them to be free and open, to express their own ideas, to show initiative in work and play. After we had heard of the visit of the Shah, each day we made a game of lining up to greet him.

Our children had worn uniforms from the day that each was soaked and scrubbed, and now each of these uniforms had to be washed, ironed, mended, lengthened to keep up with the growing child, and made ready for the big day. This is a lot of washing, ironing and mending and meant gaining the cooperation of hundreds of parents.

Of course children must scatter flowers before the feet of a king,

111

but in Dashte Moghan there were no flowers to scatter. We had worried about this until we had decided to teach the children to make paper garlands. Day after day the teachers helped sweaty little hands to shape the bright paper into something that almost resembled flowers. I had enjoyed looking into the kindergartens and seeing the little faces twisted in concentration as they created flowers for a king. The day before the flood the last garland had been completed.

For several weeks we had been learning songs to sing for the Shah. These weren't the usual childish songs. We had been asked to use special songs of greeting. Since these were difficult and in Farsi, learning them had taken special effort.

But most important of all we took time to talk about our country and about our Shah. Perhaps these children were too small to have felt the independent spirit of the tribes, to know that with many tribesmen the tribe comes even before Iran. We told them about Shah Abbas, who had chosen their own ancestors to make up his special army, and of how Iran had grown to be the Jewel of the East and Half the World. We talked to them of our own Shah and his eagerness to help the people. We showed pictures of the Shah, of the Queen, and of the little Crown Prince. Our stories were meant to give the children national pride and reverence for their ruler. That these discussions reached beyond the tents soon became clear to us when the women asked us to tell them the stories, too.

Yet I was glad that we had planned to finish our preparations early because we could forget them while we worked with the distribution of food, water and other supplies to those who were painfully beginning to dig themselves out.

I had stopped to advise a man who must have been about thirty but looked sixty or seventy who was removing the debris from the mouth of a cave in which his wife and three children had been caught and drowned. My mind was with him and I was thinking that it doesn't take ten thousand deaths to make a tragedy—one death is enough if you are close to that death—as I came toward the jeep barefoot over a sea of mud. One of the top officials from the office called to me.

"Lady Najafi, the children are to be ready to greet the Shah at seven-thirty in the morning."

"Seven-thirty? I understood he was arriving at eleven."

"He is. But the army wants everything in readiness. No mistakes."

"It will be a mistake to get the children there more than three hours before they are needed," I said grimly.

He laughed easily. "You'll manage. You can keep them entertained."

Perhaps it was his laugh that brought into my mind the memory of the gossip I had heard about this man. And, because I was exhausted by the day's work and unready to think of looking after those children so many extra hours, I said, "You must love to be with children, but why do you stay away from your home in the evenings? Why do you stay away and play games with the other men instead of going home and having fun with your children?"

He frowned, almost like a cross boy, at my words about staying home in the evenings. It was to this phrase he answered, "I am not alone in this."

"I know," I agreed. In Iran men really love their families, but one seldom sees fathers playing and romping with their children as one does in America. "But, since you are fortunate enough to have your wife and family with you, it seems that—"

"I don't like the noise of children, if you must know." His voice told me that I had put my nose into a private door. He could not stand his own children for an hour or two in the evenings and yet he thought that three and a half hours with almost five hundred of them would be a delight to us. I didn't retort but he went on uneasily, "I have too many children. My home is not peaceful. My wife always sees to the children but she has no time for me."

"And why so many children?"

He looked at me sharply. "I am not alone in this either. Our wives want many children. They feel to keep the family small is against the teachings of our religion."

"Much can be blamed on the wives," I said.

He disregarded the sarcasm of my remark. "At seven-thirty, then, at Parsabad."

Now why did I talk to him like that? His private life is certainly not my affair, I thought. I must be more unhappy than I know about getting the children there so early. And I remembered when I was about the age of these kindergarten children. I had stood with the little girls from my school through a long, long ceremony when Reza Shah, our Shah's father, had cut the ribbon that officially opened the railroad from the Caspian Sea to the Persian Gulf. The ribbon cutting was a part of a great national celebration, but to me it was nothing but a weary experience. High school girls, dressed in white and carrying baskets of flowers, filled the great Teheran station. We children stood in the streets where we could see nothing—not even the train. We stood for hours. While there were music, talking, more music, more oratory, we stood watching our flowers wilt in our damp hands and wondering if it would be polite for us to sit on the ground and rest awhile. And so I had sympathy for the children who would stand three and a half hours before anything really happened. But in the end they would see the Shah, put down their garlands for him, sing their songs. I had been invited to stand with the other officials and represent the woman's program, but I preferred to help my girls with the children.

Getting to Parsabad by seven-thirty meant getting out of bed when the first thread of dawn needled through the sky. The girls in their villages went from house to house. "Come, it is time. Wash yourself and put on your clean uniform. There will be milk and bread at the kindergarten." Then, in every home, there was the excited chirping of children, the same all over the world. I should have liked to share in the inspection of the children before the serving of the milk and bread, but I had to check on the vehicles that would carry the children to Parsabad and at Parsabad I had to make sure that the rope that would confine the children was at the right place, that there was a convenient latrine, that drinking water was available and that cookies were convenient if the children needed a distraction.

Just before seven-thirty the last load of children arrived, shouting and singing. These children were from the seven kindergartens. There were even some children whose families lived in villages 4, 5, and 6 who had stayed with relatives in order to participate in this wonderful day.

Is there anything more beautiful than a group of happy shining children all clean and neatly dressed? All of our children had bare feet, of course, but this the Shah would expect. Looking at the children I contrasted them with the dirty little urchins we had put in the barrel of warm water to soak and be scrubbed. Looking at the shining hair I thought of the millions of nits that had been conquered by the kerosene-dipped comb. Surely the tomorrows would be better for these children than the todays were for their parents.

Several of the children coaxed to hold their garlands. These, we knew, would be worn out long before the Shah arrived if the children were allowed to hold them in their hands. And I remembered how the little girl who had stood next to me when the railroad completion was celebrated had turned a fish-belly white and vomited all over herself and her handful of fading flowers.

Eight o'clock. Already the children were pushing against the ropes, running back and forth to the latrine, wandering around, looking for something to do.

Nine o'clock. The boys were beginning to push and crowd each other, not because they wanted any special place in the line but because pushing and crowding are boy activities.

Ten o'clock. In spite of the clean pressed uniforms the smaller children were lying in the dirt, some already asleep. "After all," I told one little girl who was trying her best to keep her younger brother, Siroos, from curling up in the dust, "he has been awake a long, long time." "And now he will miss the Shah entirely if he has his way," she said, shaking him until his head rolled from side to side.

Ten-thirty o'clock. We went among the children with cookies, which set half of them crying to be allowed to get a drink. Only a half an hour now. Just stand for a half hour.

Eleven o'clock. A blare of brass came to the ear. Quickly the children found their places. We passed out the garlands and small paper flags.

Eleven-ten o'clock. All ready. "There he is. There's the Shah. Oh, there he is!"

In perfect order, just as we have practiced, the garlands are laid on the ground and each child prepares to wave his flag. The Shah comes abreast and it is time to sing.

The first song is a classic written by Ashir-ad-din. This is an Arabic name meaning Light of Religion. Here is a free translation not nearly as beautiful as the poem in Farsi.

> *I am a newborn flower from the garden.*
> *In the dawn I waken to the murmur of the breezes*
> *And the murmur tells me that in this beautiful day*
> *We will welcome a very dear thing . . . a dear being.*
> *Since you are our guest today,*
> *Blessed and happy be your steps to us.*

The second song was written especially for the occasion. To the people of Iran the extravagant phrases do not seem strange.

> *Oh, King, you have come to inspect us.*

(Or perhaps this line should say, "You have come to look after us." or perhaps, "You have come to see the nation.")

> *Oh, King, you are stepping on our bodies,*
> *Your steps are on us. You are welcome.*
> *Eternal and happy be the King.*

(This is like the English phrase "Long live the King!",

> *You are welcome. Your steps be on our eyes.*
> *The descendants of Moghs from the Moghan Plains*

(Moghs are priests or wise men, something like the magi.)

> *Have become very happy, oh Shadow of God,*

(This is an ancient title of the Shah taken from the Arabic.)

> *You have brought blessings to the Moghan Plain.*

The Shah stopped while the children sang and waved their flags. Each of them saw him, and, even more important, felt that he had seen them.

It is hard for people who have grown up in a democracy to realize what our Shah means to us. Of course he has enemies as any ruler would have in his place, but to his subjects he is more than a man, he is a symbol of the country as a flag is, except animate and human. For him even the tribespeople who have no strong national spirit feel a broader stirring of love than that which they feel for friends or family, a stirring that might be called patriotism but is something indefinably different.

After the Shah had passed, the rope was let down and the children swarmed into the street, scrambling to rescue the garlands they had so lovingly laid down a few minutes before. We had rounded our little ones up and loaded them into their vehicles before the Shah returned an almost unheard-of thing—to speak to the girls and me.

"Lady Najafi." I had not expected this official introduction but I knew how to respond.

"The same Lady Najafi who worked in Baluchistan?"

My heart was jumping in my breast. The work in Baluchistan had come to his attention. Perhaps, just perhaps, that work was not dead. I did not care who carried it on as long as it went forward.

"The same," I said. And then one by one the girls were introduced, flushing with excitement and pleasure.

"I am pleased with this project. Pleased and amazed." Then he asked some questions about the kindergartens. We told him that he had been greeted by four hundred and eighty children from seven kindergartens and that the mothers and even the fathers had been brought to us by the children.

When the Shah had left us Pooran turned to me her sweet, beautiful face all radiant. "To think that I should speak with the King of Kings. This must be a fairy dream and I shall awaken."

"It isn't a dream," I told her. But I was thinking back to the first time I had seen Pooran. When I had begun my work in Sarbandan I had needed village workers and I had wanted to train them myself. I had gone to the Imperial Organization of Social Services for advice and they had allowed me to choose girls from the work center in Teheran. The work center is really a home for homeless children—orphans. Over a hundred girls had applied to return with me to Sarbandan. I had chosen three, but though two of them had begged me to choose Pooran I had looked at her poor bent back and had thought that she would be too frail for village work. Later I had brought back one of the girls who was hopelessly homesick for Teheran. Pooran had caught my hand. "My lady," she had begged, "please, please take me with you."

Standing there in the crowded general room of the work center I had said a silent prayer. "God, help me to know." And a feeling of peace wrapped around me like a spiritual chadar and I knew. "Yes, Pooran, I will take you with me." And when my two girls saw her they came running and laughing and calling, "Koocheck, Koo-check." (Little one.) Pooran had learned more rapidly than any other student I had ever had. She soon became a gifted reader, a fine needlewoman. And now she was a gracious lady.

From work center to an audience with the Shah. No wonder Pooran should now say, "That I should speak with the King of Kings."

Just as the Shah is the symbol of his country, so Pooran became to me the symbol of the progress my people can make if the opportunity is given them. Pooran was not in a dream, but perhaps I was. Perhaps this will remain a dream until all of us translate it into reality.

Homah was almost as radiant as Pooran. "Perhaps this will solve our problem with the Department of Education. Perhaps now the Shah will speak for us."

"I do not know," I said, as this worrisome question wiped away the vision I had been enjoying. "Perhaps he will feel that our kindergartens are exactly what the Department of Education needs."

By afternoon we had put the ceremony of the Shah's visit behind us. The children were back safely with their mothers, and never would they be done talking about the handsome, smiling Shah, the music, the soldiers, the special cookies, and the garlands that they could keep forever if they took good care of them.

In my rooms I quickly checked with Nassim, Ramazan and Nannie. I had scarcely seen my baby since the first hour of the flood. I put on my sturdiest clothing, tied a scarf over my head and picked up my sheepskin-lined jacket. "It will be late again when I come home. See that Nassim is fed and clean and in her bed early."

It was easier to get around now. The mud was solidifying and we could go part way by jeep. And there was still much to be done.

When I think now of the flood I think first of the Mullah who wakened the people from their shock and set them to helping themselves through work and prayer. I think of the funeral processions moving through ankle-deep, sometimes knee-deep mud, to the raw new cemetery. I think of passing out drinking water in pitiful little cupfuls and having that shared so that the bodies of the dead might be washed. But more poignant than these memories are those of a sharp-boned old man I saw the afternoon of the Shah's visit. He was sitting in the mud, the decaying body of a sheep across his knees. He was trying to cut the wool from the animal. The burial squad should long since have put this carcass in the earth; the smell of rotting flesh was almost unbearable, but the old man looked up at me with trust in his eyes, mixed somehow with pain and hopelessness. "This sheep, she used to give my grandchildren milk and cheese and yogurt. She used to give us a new lamb each year. Now I must take from her her last gift." I knew that I must order the animal buried at once, but I turned away with sudden tears. Many years before Dr. Birjandi had told me that I must educate my heart to be hard. This I had never been able to do.

It was ten days before clear drinking water was again available in all of the villages. Until that time water had to be carried in great tankers and distributed a jar at a time. It was more than ten days before all of the dead animals were buried and the debris cleared from the villages. It was still longer before the people began to build new shelters to take the place of the flimsy structures that had been washed away by the flood.

And, for many, things would never be the same again. They had lost not only tangible things but their faith in their government. This would never have happened to them if it hadn't been for us, the people the government had trusted to guide them.

10 ❖ The Building

AT LAST THE HORROR WAS OVER. NOT THE SADNESS, NOT THE DISIL-
lusionment of the people in the government resettling and land
program, not the tears for the dead; but the acute suffering, the
reaching out of a shaking hand for a single cup of water, the de-
spairing efforts to cleanse a carpet which had been the beautiful
possession of a family for generations, or the search through piles of
debris for a beloved samovar that had been swirled away by the
flood. The wall of water had swept away not only the possessions of
the people of the three new villages, but their spirit as well.

Red-eyed and half unconscious from lack of sleep, Pahvine and I
fell into bed and slept the clock around. When I awakened there
was a message from Malak Mansoor. He wished to see me as soon as
possible.

Even under these pressures we greeted each other with the usual
Persian civilities. He thanked me for the work that Pahvine and I
had accomplished. He especially thanked us for the responsibility
we took the first day after the flood. Then his face grew sober and I
knew that this was not just a mutual-congratulation conference.

"There is yet much to be done."

"Yes," I answered.

"The physical things. We can safely leave those to the engineers.
The spiritual things. You will know how to handle those."

I thought of the first day that we were in Bampoor. We had held
a meeting in the new garden of the Agricultural Department. The
people had sat and listened to the whine of the mosquito until they
were weary. They heard little of the beautiful, inspiring speech that

121

had been prepared for them.

"The spirit must be born from inside each person," I said. "I must work with the head men from the villages. The work must be done little by little."

Then Malak Mansoor used one of my own phrases, "Heart by heart, Najmeh."

Pooran took over my routine work while I went about talking with the people. I allowed them to tell me of their disappointments, of their problems. Only by telling these things would they be relieved of the weight of their grievances. Once when I was a child I stepped barefooted upon a worn wooden floor. I knew that I had hurt my foot. I hopped around on the other foot until my mother grew weary with my new game. Then my foot began to swell and the whole foot and leg were red and painful. My nannie had washed it with light careful strokes, but finally Mohsen said, "Let me see." He took my foot and pushed at the flesh around the angry spot; a splinter popped out.

Now, working with gentleness and yet with honesty, I must probe around the sore spot until the splinter popped out and left the heart a chance to heal. With the head men of the villages I discussed village problems. I discussed national problems, too. But mostly they did the talking. I tried to help them to decide for themselves that they could handle the problems that a new sort of settled life would bring them. I was an instructor in rural government, in rural sociology, in psychology, even in religion, and all this I had to do with few words.

April passed into May. In Teheran there had been a change of premiers. Ali Amini had been given extraordinary powers a year before but he had not been able to halt the decline of Iran toward bankruptcy. We did not know how long the missions to Dashte Moghan would last in the pressure for economy so we hurried our work to prepare the wiser people of the village to take over if and when that was necessary.

June, and the people were growing restless. The trek to the mountains began. This year fewer would go, but still no one could foresee the date of the last migration. And with the beginning of the move to the summer grasslands came a change for me. I received word that CARE had asked the government to lend me to them for three months. This could mean but one thing. CARE was ready to build the factory in Sarbandan. All during the flood and the heart-breaking days that followed it I had scarcely thought of Sarbandan, but now I was jubilant. Close upon this news came word that Shapoor had almost finished his European tour and would be back in Teheran almost as soon as I would be.

Pooran would take over my work while I was away. She was capable, well-trained, respected, even loved. I would not need to worry.

I did not know until I was packed and on my way back to Teheran with Nassim, Ramazan and Nannie how depressing the Dashte Moghan experience had been. True, there had been the kindergartens, the joy of seeing the women come to us and ask for instruction, but though I had been smiling, speaking words of comfort or of encouragement, inside I had been dark and weighted with lead. But I was going home. Home to Sarbandan, to Shapoor, to Sina, to the Najmeh that was entirely woman.

In Teheran I went at once to Mohsen's, where my mother now made her home. I would not stay there long. Shapoor and I must have our own home. I began to look for something I could buy and furnish. "Why don't you wait until Shapoor comes home?" my family asked. They could not know the adjustment that one must make coming from America back to Teheran. When he arrived in Teheran things should be comfortable for him. He should not be reminded that he was just beginning a life again.

Finally I found the house—a little house in a new neighborhood. In America you would say a tract house, but our houses are different. Each one has a front garden and a pool (not a swimming pool as in America, but a mirror pool to decorate the garden and add coolness), and a paved back court. And, yes, each is surrounded by a wall. This is a wall that can be jumped over by a man, but it still gives the feeling of privacy that had seemed to me to be lacking in American subdivisions.

The house, made of stucco and not at all beautiful, was not in the old city, but nearer the mountains. One could reach the center of Teheran by taking a taxi to Fouziah Square and then another taxi from there to the government center. But this would not be difficult and taxis are inexpensive. Of course there was a bus from Fouziah Square, but the buses are crowded, dirty and sometimes unsafe.

Our little house had many rooms, most of them small. On one side of a central hall there was a long living room that could be decorated to be gracious and charming, and behind it a kitchen and leading from a hall a room for the servants and a small double room containing a latrine, Persian version, and a wash basin. On the other side of the hall were four small bedrooms. Two of these, on the front of the house, I had made into one larger room with a curtain where the wall would have originally been. Open, this would be the family room. Closed it would be a bedroom for each of the children. The bedroom at the back would be mine—ours. . . .

Between the family room and the back bedroom I would have a stone-floored room with a shower. Of course I would still take my family and my servants to the public bath once a week; this is something that must be done, but for the daily bath we would have the shower. I was filled with plans for the new home; eager to buy several colors of chiffon to drape the windows; anxious to select carpets. Mohsen had offered a choice and I was considering pale green carpets with realistic flower borders rather than the conventional Persian carpets. I gathered one piece of furniture here, another there, from pieces my brothers and sisters had set aside as no longer suitable for their use.

All this I was doing while I was beginning my work with CARE. Now that the factory was actually possible I was burning with energy. We asked the Ministry of Roads to level the ground, PLAN to draw a building plan the engineers felt would be suitable. After careful study we decided that the equipment should be purchased from Canada and CARE placed the order. PLAN signed an agreement with CARE that when the Sarbandan factory was completed the organization would help with needed raw material. All of these arrangements took endless meetings, endless correspondence, endless investigation and study.

Often I took Mother, the children, the servants and went to Sarbandan for a quiet Friday. Since the doctor and his wife had moved to Teheran I had left a couple in charge of our sweet house but they had found it too large for themselves and their five sons. I built a strong room connected to the back wall and in this one room they felt comfortable. Whenever I took my family to Sarbandan the house waited for me.

Early one morning, before even Nassim and Sina were awake, I dressed in my village clothes and followed the jube through the quiet village street. Already many women were filling their water jugs and they spoke to me as I went by. Then I turned off from the street with the jube and climbed up over the foothills to the land where the factory would stand. This was still a quiet place to sit and pray, or just to sit.

I thought of the dream that was soon to unwind into reality. It is not everybody who finds a dream coming true in his own lifetime. Years ago, when I was a young girl, and before I had ever been to America, I had opened a dress shop in the old quarter of Teheran. Not a dress shop in the American sense, but a dress shop where custom-made clothes were designed and executed for special people. In the window of the shop I had very simple decoration. Perhaps a piece of chiffon draped gracefully and on it a single brooch. Perhaps gloves, resting on a handbag. Perhaps a single gown, not on a manikin but draped across a bench. My goods were not in the window. What was shown was good taste.

In the front room of my shop there were chairs for my clients, a soft carpet and style books from Paris. In the back room several girls sat at sewing machines making the dresses that I had designed. These girls I had taken from the streets of Teheran. They were sometimes girls without hope, girls without background. And every day I turned away girls who had heard of the shop and wished to learn and work. I had thought then that all that stood between the girls of Iran and the good life was a chance to work, and I had dreamed of a factory in which more girls could be employed.

Because of this dream I had gone to America. I had not prepared myself with a single word of English so I lost some time before I began to work seriously on the study of design at Pasadena City College and of factory machines at the Los Angeles Trade and Technical College. From the first I had dreamed that from native materials a factory might turn out dresses that would be inexpensive enough for poor people to wear. I had dreamed of making medium-priced garments for those who could not afford custom-made garments of the modiste shops like mine.

And then I had met Eleanor Roosevelt. In a country like Iran, she said, where there is less employment, less hurry, women should be taught to make their own clothing. What is really needed is less expensive and better materials. A weaving factory would be a better project than a garment factory. In the village I had discovered that every woman could learn to dress herself and her family if she was given instructions in cutting and sewing.

Now, sitting on the site that the village had given for the factory, I put the two dreams together. Perhaps someday we would make material on our own looms and in our sewing rooms use it to work out our own designs.

When I walked back through the village the men were gathering near the teahouse. "When will we have another meeting, Lady Najafi?" Kutchiki, the short Kadkhoda, asked.

"Very soon. Next week, perhaps. I will bring an expert with me from Teheran."

The next week, sitting in the teahouse of Mash'hadi Mokhtar, I introduced the CARE representative to the important men of the village. But still the men wanted me to speak. They had learned to bring their problems to me, and when I was there they felt that even the dehyars sent by the government should listen to my words. It was awkward, but he understood. Now we talked about what part of the work the village men could do. All of it, they thought, and they pointed to the clinic that they had raised with their own hands. We should start with the wall, I suggested. On the wall we could show the experts from CARE which men knew how to build, which could be trusted to build straight and true and according to directions. Straight and true, I thought, but hardly according to directions. When I had employed workmen to remodel the house I made into the first village center and school I had found that following directions is the last thing a Persian workman wants to do.

What was the pay for working on these walls? Would there be more stock in the factory?

No, I said, and explained to them CARE's plan—a plan for reaching the needy without destroying their pride. "You all have flour at home," I told them. "Every day your wife can bake the bread for your family. You all have plenty of cooking oil. You have milk for your children." These things I told them though they were not all true. "But in every home there is need for more of these things. It is up to you to select men to build the wall who know how to work. They should also be men who have families and need food for these families."

Then I passed around the circle of silent men pictures of CARE products: sacks of grain, cans of cooking oil, cartons of dried milk. I translated for them the words on these packages. "This is not for sale. A gift of the American people."

It is hard for the people of my country to understand that in America more is produced than can be used; that there are actually "surplus products." In a land where famine waits on every street, "surplus" is a difficult word to translate. I told them of the food in the government storehouses in America. I told them how CARE, getting money from thousands of kind-hearted Americans, was able to take this surplus food from the American government and bring it to countries like Iran, where there was hunger. Then I explained how the Red Lion and Sun, our Red Cross, brings it from the seaport to the area where it is needed.

As I talked of these things my heart reached out toward America —her clean streets, her clean, well-dressed people, but specially for the kind hearts I found wherever I went in that country. And foolishly I felt tears in my eyes.

There was another meeting, another and another, before these important men in the village had selected the men that should work on the wall and perhaps on the factory.

"He is a good man," Old Massud, drawing on his hubbly-bubbly, said of his own nephew. "But he is a vegetable."

"He is a good worker," Mash'hadi Mokhtar said of another, "but he has a wasteful wife. She throws more to the chickens than he can carry in his door."

"He is a good man, but . . ." And so these men gave careful consideration to one man at a time until all had been discussed. Then they gave the dehyar, Mr. Nadaff, the names to write down for builders of the wall.

Now my work in the village was completed for a time. As Mr. Nadaff returned me to Teheran he said, "Do you have copies of your speeches?"

"Speeches?"

"Yes, for example the speech on cooperation."

"Oh, those. I have outlines for those speeches."

"Will you write those speeches and give them to me? Many times I can read them to the men when the need arises."

"You can yourself say whatever is needful."

"Your words will be better," he insisted. And so I wrote some speeches and gave them to him. The villagers would hear my words if not my voice if difficulties arose.

Back in Teheran I conferred with CARE about the factory. The big weaving room would hold sixteen large looms. There would be a room for stretching and drying, one for dyeing, and one for sewing. CARE had built other factories like this and they were more experienced than I. I was representing the stockholders in these conferences. I smiled to think of these simple villagers as capitalists, but in exchange for their land they had received shares in the factory.

In all of my spare time I watched our own house grow. I wished that Shapoor and I were completing this together, but I wanted it ready when he returned.

At last we received the wire, "Home," and he gave the day, the hour and the flight number. He had wanted to drive home in the Chevrolet he had bought with such pride in America, but by letter we had decided that would not be wise. He was flying, and Nassim and Sina and I could scarcely wait for this great bird to settle at the airport. Nassim had never seen her father. Sina thought he could remember him, but this I doubted. Shapoor's mother and father and his brothers and sisters were as eager as I.

As I hurried to get the last length of chiffon hung at my windows, Fahkri said to me, "Najmeh, you must not be disappointed."

"Disappointed?"

"Yes. You have been apart for a long time. When people are together they grow together. When they are apart they grow apart."

"That sounds wise," I said, "but I hope it is wrong."

Could Fahkri know that I had been worrying about the same thing? For days together—like the flood period in Dashte Moghan— I had not thought once of Shapoor, and I knew that there must have been days when he hadn't thought of me.

But I comforted myself that now we both had a background in America. We both could see Iran through comparison and contrast with other parts of the world.

"It was easy to leave Sina with his grandmother," Fahkri said, "but it will not be so easy to leave Shapoor in his mother's house."

"But he will have this house," I protested.

"A house without a wife is a body without a soul," she quoted an old Persian proverb. After a moment she said, "Perhaps now you will give up this work on the edge of the earth."

I had been thinking of this, too. "I don't know, Fahkri," I said in the same thoughtful way she had spoken. "When I married I did not look ahead to this conflict."

I knew that since I was needed in Dashte Moghan Malak Mansoor would find a place for Shapoor there. Dr. Birjandi would have found a place for him in Bampoor. But a man must find his own place. Shapoor was not even home yet and I was being stretched apart.

"The woman's place is in the home," Fahkri said.

"That is what is said all over the world," I retorted.

"It's said all over the world because it is true."

We waited outside the airport, looking through the windows, for Shapoor to arrive, for him to go through customs. We were all there, his family, mine, the children. There were flowers in every room of our new house and a brother-in-law was lending us a car so we could drive to our own home as soon as the greetings were over.

At last there he was, looking thinner, a little paler, a little more bald, perhaps, than I had remembered, but with the same abrupt radiance in his face as he saw us waiting there for him.

Both children clambered to be lifted up while we waited for him to go through customs. Then at last there he was. He kissed me briefly and tousled the hairdo I had had just for him. Then he lifted Sina. With Sina's legs wrapped around his body, Shapoor greeted each member of his family, then my family, then turned to me.

"You haven't greeted Nassim," I said, some of the baby's hurt at being neglected shadowing my voice.

"She's a beautiful child, Najmeh," Shapoor said, and he kissed her, but even as he did so his eyes were on Sina.

Why, he doesn't feel as if Nassim was his child at all, I thought.

"Come to our home," his mother suggested. "There is so much we want to hear about your trip and about your school."

I looked at her with some surprise. I thought that all of the family knew that I had counted on Shapoor's coming straight to our new home.

"Good," Shapoor answered heartily. Then as an afterthought, "How about it, Najmeh?"

Of course I said, "Yes," and we went to the home of his sister, where the family had prepared a great dinner of all the food that he would have missed most during his stay in America. When he was talking with his family his eyes were shining and his face flushed with excitement. I thought, I am almost a stranger—an outsider. And at times I saw his eyes on me with a scarcely veiled look of puzzlement. The night of our marriage I had left our home to help to take care of a man whose abdomen had been slit in a fight and Shapoor had said, "Najmeh-jun, I sometimes wonder what I married." And now I felt that his eyes were saying the same thing.

The children grew tired and cross and I put them to bed on borrowed beds, but still the laughter and conversation went on. It was very late when he at last called a taxi to drive us to our own home.

"The home is just as you wrote me," he said when we opened the front door and carried the children into their rooms. I thought he took it too much for granted. He undressed Sina and put him to bed while I cared for Nassim. "Sina is Daddy's boy," he said over and over in his soothing way as he took care of our son. I knew how much he had missed his son and tried not to wonder how much he had missed me.

I took almost a week off to visit with Shapoor since he must call on all of his friends in order not to lose them. At the end of the week I was glad to go back to my office at CARE; glad to take Shapoor back to Sarbandan to see the progress of the factory.

Shapoor was more interested in the wheat field in front of our Sarbandan house than he was in the factory. It was just beginning to turn yellow and he was fascinated. "It's pure gold, Najmeh-jun," he said over and over again. "One man with an American tractor could cultivate all of these fields."

"Do you think of turning farmer?" I teased him.

"Of course not. No. I am an office worker. I plan to work for the government."

Together we walked up to the place where the factory was being built. In America we had walked often with my arm through his, or perhaps with our little fingers linked in a special way we had, but in Iran we walked apart. Even a husband and wife must not show affection in public.

I was surprised at how rapidly the building had progressed. I had thought that it would be built entirely by our villagers but skilled workers had been brought from Teheran and the villagers stood by and watched the work progress. To them it was a very fine building, from its concrete foundation to its corrugated metal roof shining in the sun. There was no one reluctant to take the credit for being one of the first to offer land for such a building; no one who did not comment on his own ability to cooperate in bringing such a structure to our village.

For a time the beautiful building stood empty waiting for the looms. I was in my CARE office when word came that the looms were in the harbor at Khorramshahr. I was ecstatic! And then a simple problem arose—the sort of problem that is always jumping out at me. CARE had paid for shipping the looms to Khorramshahr; the Red Lion and Sun had budgeted the money to bring the looms from Khorramshahr to Teheran; the Imperial Organization of Social Services would transport the looms from Teheran to Sarbandan. How simple everything sounded. But who would unload the looms from the ship and load them on the trucks? Who would make the transfer to Teheran? Who would unload the trucks and carry in the looms at Sarbandan? For these jobs no money had been appropriated.

"What will you do, Najmeh?" Shapoor asked curiously when I told him that looms were in the harbor but were tied up by this problem. Khorramshahr! I couldn't possibly go that distance to untangle matters.

"With the looms so close how can I give up?"

Shapoor, long enough in America to forget how to use common transportation, was missing his beloved Chevrolet. "We must get a car, Najmeh," he insisted. How could I think of a car while the looms were stranded in the harbor?

"A Volkswagen will do," he insisted.

And so we got a Volkswagen and Shapoor drove me to Sarbandan.

Again there was a meeting of the stockholders in the factory.

"The looms are in the harbor," I told them. They nodded contentedly, smiled, then drew upon their pipes.

"There they will stay," I said sadly.

Then I explained the oversight that had not provided for fees for longshoremen. "We must pay to have these looms moved from ship to truck," I said.

Mash'hadi Mohktar always seemed to smell my requests for money even before I made them.

"This factory was to make money, Lady Najafi. Why does it day by day take money?"

The other men nodded. But now that the question was open I leaned forward so I could see the other faces in the lantern light.

"You all have stock in this factory. If it makes money then you share that money. If it stands empty how can anybody profit?"

The men moved restlessly but finally the tall Kadkhoda said, "How much money will be required?"

"These are the estimates," I said, and even the villagers who cannot read strained forward to see.

"I will give; but this will be the last time," Mash'hadi Mokhtar said. Following his lead the others agreed.

Shapoor took me back to the city. In the coziness of the Volkswagen he said quietly, "Najmeh, do you always get what you want?" When I was quiet he went on. "You got those men to do what you wanted them to do."

I remembered that he had sat on the edge of the circle with not a word to say. I was tired from the encounter, concerned about the looms, and perhaps I was a little sharp. "I wasn't asking anything for myself."

Shapoor persisted. "In a way you were asking something for yourself. That factory is more than a public service for the village. It is a very real part of your life."

"Yes," I agreed.

"And so you were asking that they help to bring your dreams to fruitfulness. Isn't that so?"

"Perhaps." Then I turned to him and put my arm through his so that I could feel his muscles tense as he gripped the wheel. "Why are you saying these things to me?"

He didn't answer my question. "You know if you handle each situation wisely they will give you what you want."

Again I asked, "Why are we talking this way, Shapoor? We have been apart for so long that we should use this time to learn to know each other all over again."

"I wonder, Najmeh, if you are trying to handle me."

I was silent. I, myself, didn't know the answer to this question.

At last the looms were unloaded at the factory while everyone in the village watched. I had told them that the looms would arrive in a condition the Americans call "knocked-down," but I think they had not believed me. The men, women and children watched until every piece was taken inside the factory.

"Is this all?" one of the young men asked me.

"Soon an engineer will come and set up the looms. Then you will see."

An engineer trained by the Germans under Reza Shah came to the village to set up the looms with a hundred pair of eyes on him at all times. "Sar Reshtah can do this thing without our help," I told the people; but still there was something good in their curiosity and interest. At the end of the month all sixteen looms were up and in running order.

Perhaps in America an enterprise like this would begin to make money at once. This we didn't expect. First the girls and women must learn how to produce a usable product; to do this we must have an instructor. Mr. Monjzeh, who had helped to plan the factory, suggested that we bring a teacher from Tabriz.

Again all of the village turned out to look at him when he arrived. He was an ugly giant wth a huge nose, enormous nostrils, small eyes. To look at him made me sick. And to smell him was even worse since he was dirty. There was no home for him near the factory so I took him into my house. Night and day I burned incense. Incense doesn't destroy an offensive odor, it merely masks it. When the instructor left I would burn his bedding, everything that had touched him.

"Why does God send me such ugly men?" I asked Shapoor. He only laughed and I began to realize that when I was working with men Shapoor preferred them old or ugly.

Who should be first to learn weaving from this man? All of the girls and women in the village wanted to be employed in the factory. Why should work be denied them? they asked. All those who had stock in the factory insisted on work there as a right not a privilege.

I sat hour after hour writing the names of the girls and women who wanted to work. It was my idea that as many of the girls as possible should learn to operate the looms; in this way there would always be a labor supply. Nadaff watched me register the girls.

"I must make a suggestion," he said. "We should train one girl from each family."

"Some girls will weave as easily as a spider. Others will weave as easily as a frog," I told him.

"But the fruits of the factory must be extended to everyone," he argued.

Then I tried to explain to him that in order to share the value of a medical clinic each person in the village must have an equal right to take their illnesses there. But with the factory things would be different. When a woman works in the factory she has more money to buy sugar at the food store. Money for shoelaces or even for shoes at the notions store. Money for some sweet herbs at the apothecary's. And perhaps she will have money to pay some other girl or woman to look after her children.

Nadaff shook his head. These fundamental lessons in economics were not for him.

For a time the looms stood idle while the girls on the register worried and the old men shook their heads as they smoked their pipes in the teahouse. Finally the lists of girls and women who were to be the first to learn were completed.

It was a day for celebrating the morning that we took our places at the looms, for I learned with the others.

The teacher was a giant and he was ugly. I soon heard that he never went to the mosque so he must be an atheist; that he stole bobbins so he must be dishonest; all sorts of rumors. But he was an excellent teacher and the girls, watching every movement he made, finally made the looms sing as they worked.

"You are quick to learn," he told me, and I was pleased, though it was not strange that a woman who had used machines for many years should have more facility than one who had never before seen anything mechanical.

There was argument among the men, too. Who should be the manager of the factory? Who should be the watchman? Who should learn to repair the looms?

Always I was worried. CARE had built the factory with the promise that PLAN would take it over. Yet no one in PLAN seemed interested. If Shapoor thought that I got everything I asked for he should have followed me from one office to another trying to get a hearing on the factory.

The time was getting close when I would need to return to Dashte Moghan. I spoke little of this to Shapoor; but to Mash'hadi Mokhtar, and later to both Kadkhodas, I spoke often. Always I said the same thing. "The factory is fine. But I would be happy if you could finish the organization of the cooperative before I leave."

"We will consider it," they always promised.

My work at the office of CARE was completed so we remained in Sarbandan. The children loved life in the village. A village is the safest place in the world. Every child looks after all of the smaller children, so Sina and Nassim could roam, get dirty, go barefooted, make friends with everybody. They loved the evening when the candle lighted them to bed and Shapoor was there to tell stories to Sina to which Nassim listened, half comprehending, but completely worshipful.

Often I sat in the teahouse of Mash'hadi Mokhtar while the hubbly-bubblies made their soft murmuring and listened to the half-silence while the men gave consideration to the suggestions that had been made. Three days before I had to return to Teheran the operations were completed, the agreements finished, Sarbandan had a cooperative. All that remained now was to register it.

"Now you have everything you want for Sarbandan," Shapoor told me.

"Not everything. The clinic is unsatisfactory and the government will not change the doctor. The girls have outgrown their schoolroom; they should have two teachers instead of one. The women are learning to weave and we have the looms and the factory but as yet we do not have materials to begin work, nor contracts for the material we produce."

Shapoor lifted his hands in an exasperating shrug. "Poor Najmeh. Poor Najmeh-jun."

I I ❖ Again Winter

THE END OF AUGUST WAS APPROACHING AND THE SUMMER HAD
run like a jube past my door. Always in Sarbandan I had been fascinated by the life on the banks of the jube. On the edge of this
running water there are work, play, sorrow, happiness, and here the
people drink deeply of the satisfying draught of life. The summer,
like a jube, had brought me everything: Shapoor home from America, a life as a family in our new little home, the completion of the
factory building in Sarbandan, a deep, satisfying sense of accomplishment. Often as I lay in my bed and listened to the night
breathing of my family I thought, "How comforting these sounds
are to a mother." And I hesitated to pack my suitcase and leave for
the North. Yet CARE had borrowed me for three months and now it
was time to return to Dashte Moghan.

Perhaps I had allowed myself to hope that Shapoor would find a
position in the Dashte Moghan project—several of the engineers
had their wives and families with them—but he had already found
a government position that would keep him in Teheran.

As I lay wide-eyed in the darkness I thought, *I cannot understand
myself. To me this home is the safest, sweetest place on earth, and
yet I am anxious, even eager, to get back to Dashte Moghan and
continue with the projects we have begun.*

Shapoor said little about my going, but it seemed to me that he
spent less time with me as the time for my departure grew nearer.
My sisters told me again and again, "You can't go out from your
husband as you did from Sina. A proper wife does not go out from
her home." And I heard that Shapoor's family, especially his

mother, felt that I was a poor wife indeed.

In September when the nomads came back from the mountains all of my girls greeted me in Alirezabad. My eyes had longed for each face and I was like a mother greeting her children. At once innumerable problems were piled in my lap.

The government was in serious financial trouble and the program at Dashte Moghan as well as everywhere else had been curtailed as an economy measure. I insisted that as long as the government could pay the salaries of the girls we would keep our entire program running. Materials? We would use our ingenuity. The need for a larger staff? We would work longer hours.

One of the engineers stopped me one morning as I was going toward the kindergarten. "Lady Najafi," he said, "I want to talk to you. Did you know that you are making life harder for all of us? This is what they tell me, 'If Lady Najafi can work twelve hours, why not you?' "

"I will do my overtime work in my room," I promised. "But look across the border. In fifteen minutes you could be in Russia, only you haven't permission to go. But the eye can go into Russia in less than fifteen minutes. I look and my eye is there now. And so are the eyes of the Shahsavans."

"Can I help it if my country is bankrupt?" he asked and turned and walked away.

The growing children needed new uniforms and if not uniforms at least something to cover them. The women in the sewing classes needed material to work on. We took the curtains from our windows, although the material was sun-faded and weakened, and the women made clothing for the children.

When I wrote of our problems Shapoor replied, "You could give up and come home."

I could not explain to him that we were under a special obligation to these women. They had been happy in poverty and ignorance, but we had introduced them to a new way of life. We wouldn't wish them to again be ignorant, with the high infant mortality rate, the short adult life expectancy, the superstitions that took the place of logic and clouded the mind with fear.

We taught the children to make little gardens, even though the water had to be carried in empty kerosene cans. "Only when one loves the soil and cares for it will it give tender carrots and radishes," we told the children; and the women in the classes grew interested. Yet there was murmuring. Even when we heard in Dashte Moghan that the Shah had begun his land reform program with the presentation of deed to 530 families there was murmuring. All of the nomads who would settle on the plains and send their flocks to the mountains with shepherds, instead of following them with their entire families, would soon own land. But what use was landownership if in spite of it there was still need? Why trade freedom for permanence when the settled life was not all fruit and honey?

Just when we were immersed most deeply in our problems I received an invitation to come to Teheran to consult with the Red Lion and Sun about another woman's program. When I was packed and ready to leave, Pooran put her arms around me. "This is the end of something," she said. "We never will work together again."

"I'll be gone for less than a month," I told her.

"I have a feeling," she said and turned away.

I had a feeling, too, though I didn't know how or why fate was changing this pattern.

Something had ended. I did not know until much later that Shapoor had insisted that I be released from my contract and return to Teheran.

"Just leave me here," I told the driver of the station wagon who had brought me to Sarbandan.

I had been driving toward Teheran when I had the strange feeling that I should go at once to Sarbandan. I talked with my driver about this strange extra sense that prompts a mother to recognize when a child, far away from her, is in danger. This same sense now told me that I was needed urgently in my village.

"I'll take you straight up there," the driver offered. "How far is it?" When I told him he shrugged. "What is that distance after driving from Dashte Moghan?"

"But I must first stop at my home in Teheran," I told him.

"Yes, yes, yes," he agreed, accustomed to women's vagaries.

When I stopped at my home Shapoor was not there, but my mother had filled the house with fresh flowers. I left Nassim with her but Sina begged to come with me. Hurriedly I threw some of his clothing into a suitcase and left a note for Shapoor. I had seen so little of my son. When Shapoor was at home he and Sina made a tight little team that somehow shut me, as well as Nassim, out of their special world. Now, both laughing and merry at a chance for an adventure together, we climbed into the station wagon.

Sina chattered on about the winter, his face shining, his brown eyes holding mine in a half-worshipful gaze. It was not that I hadn't seen my family. I had been home several times for two or three days, trying to keep my own personal relationships in running order— but Sina had had little chance to tell me about his own little-boy world.

It was dark long before we reached Sarbandan. The shops were, of course, closed and I had brought no food with me. "You may leave me at the teahouse," I said. "See, a light is burning there."

He put Sina and me off at the teahouse of Mash'hadi Mokhtar; then he turned and drove back to Teheran. We hesitated only a moment before I lifted Sina so that he could ring the brass bell. Musi came and let us in. He found a place for us in the light of the lantern but he didn't offer us tea.

"How are things in Sarbandan?" I asked him.

"Lady Najafi, it is too late for discussion."

"May I have some milk for my son?"

"Milk? Yes." In a few minutes he was back with bread and cheese and milk for both of us. We had supper together on the floor.

"May I light you to your home?" Musi asked, but without enthusiasm.

"No. Sina and I know every pebble." I took Sina's hand and my suitcase and went out into the sleeping night. "What makes the moon, Mama?" Sina asked, and I wondered as I gave him a half-fanciful answer who was answering his questions these months I was away.

How strange yet pleasant it was to sleep with my arm around Sina's sturdy little body. He had been a chubby baby but now he was beginning to grow slender and I felt the loss of his baby softness.

At five when I arose to pray I looked outside and saw a crowd of village men waiting on the path to my house. Hurriedly I dressed and went out to where they were waiting.

"Lady Najafi," the tall Kadkhoda said, "we have had a flood."

"Three days and everything is gone," Mash'hadi Mokhtar said, the absence of his gold crown scarcely showing through the grim set of his lips.

"Water, food, seed," the Kadkhoda said.

"What have you done?"

"Nothing."

"But why have you done nothing?"

"We were waiting for you."

"Well," I said, "you might have waited for a long time."

"It is No Ruz. You come at No Ruz. We prayed that you would come."

I remembered my telling the driver that I had a peculiar feeling that Sarbandan needed me. "Prayers are good," I said. "But in case of floods so are shovels."

I went back into my home, roused Sina, helped him to dress, and then I put on my sturdiest shoes. "We must investigate," I told the men, and with Sina by the hand I began to lead this strange procession up the road through the center of the village.

"I'm tired," Sina said almost at once, a little cross from having been wakened from a sound sleep.

"I'll carry the boy," the tall Kadkhoda said; so he lifted Sina to his shoulder.

Although it was early, others were already out on the road.

"Lady Najafi, my home is gone," a woman named Ashtar cried, clinging to me. "My home is gone. Do you hear me?"

"I hear you, Ashtar," I said. "We must control the water before we can think of our homes."

"Lady Najafi, come and see what the waters have done to my

home," another wailed, lifting her hands to me.

I thought of the flood that had swept away villages 4, 5, and 6 in Dashte Moghan and almost said, "This is a little flood. It is nothing." But I put a hook on my mouth, remembering that, if a flood washes away everything that you have though that everything is small, you are left as poor as if you had been rich and the flood had washed away all of your riches. A man can lose no more than everything that he has.

"We will see these things later," I promised. "But now—"

"How can we control the water?"

"We must see," I said. We pushed on, climbing above the village for three miles or more. I was not an engineer but I could see what needed to be done. "Everybody must work," I said.

Surprisingly Mash'hadi Mokhtar handed me a megaphone. I took it and shouted through it. "Everybody bring a shovel. In the name of Ali."

A wonderful old woman who handled a shovel like a young man reminded me, "It is difficult to work when we are empty. What shall we do for food?"

I turned to the brother of Mash'hadi Mokhtar. "Take your truck to Teheran and go to the place of my brother Mohsen in the bazaar. Tell him, 'Your sister Najmeh needs two hundred long loaves of bread.' "

"And he will give it to me?" the young man asked incredulously.

"If I say that I need he will give," I told him. "Now be fast, but do not risk your neck by being too fast. When you return bring the food to the top of the mountain." Then I turned to Mash'hadi Mokhtar, who had taken a turn carrying Sina and was still stretching his arms to relax them. "Send another brother to your teahouse and have him bring all of the bread and tea you have there."

"But, Lady Najafi," he protested.

"If my brother Mohsen who is a stranger can give two hundred loaves perhaps you can give twenty and some tea."

"You are right," he agreed.

By ten Mash'hadi Mokhtar's brother was back with the food

supplies from the teahouse and we made tea for all of those who were working.

A flash flood had filled the stream bed of the jube with debris. The first work was to clear these sticks and stones away. With all of the men and many of the women working, we would find the job a light one.

It was shortly after noon when the truck arrived with the bread from Mohsen. Mohsen had also sent rice, because many villagers think that it is impossible to live without rice. Dinner was like a great town picnic. A sheep had been killed and prepared earlier in the morning. Now all of the workers could eat mutton, bread and rice. A banquet.

By dusk half the work was completed. There was not yet water in the village, but there was clear water at the source of the jube and it could be carried to the village by the women while the men worked on the stream bed. Asghar did not work with the shovel; he prepared the food. Supper was rice and bread and soup made from the bones of the sheep and from some spring greens.

The next morning half the men started clearing the bed of the jube in the village; half worked on the mountain where we had stopped the night before. At the end of the day the jube's old bed was cleared and all that was left to do was to redirect the stream into it. When the flash flood had come it had first washed over the lower part of the village, then the debris, carried by the water, had blocked the lower stream bed and the water had found a new channel into a hidden valley. Now we blocked that course and sent the water down the jube. Everyone sang and danced with the coming of the water. It had been beautiful to see the cooperative effort.

Before I returned to Teheran I talked with the village council about the jube. Perhaps the flood would not have caused much damage had the stream bed been deep and clean. A mirab, a watermaster, should be appointed to keep debris away from the stream's source. The men nodded gravely. The flood had spoken much more loudly than the words of the dehyar. Rebuilding was begun on the houses, those whose houses had not been touched helping those who had been left homeless.

In Teheran I arranged with CARE to see the people over this emergency. When I tried to thank Mohsen for the two hundred loaves of bread the tears drowned my throat and I could not speak. Mohsen has a beautiful, loving wife, and I have a husband who loves and appreciates me. But never will wife or husband have the deep understanding that exists between Mohsen and me. It is as if we are the same cloth sewed into different garments.

The next time I went to the village Shapoor and the children were with me. Shapoor and I walked through the village, checking on the rebuilding of homes that had been destroyed or damaged by the flood. We noticed that higher on the hills, behind the cherry and apricot orchards, there were several new homes—not homes built since the flood, but homes that had probably been built in the past year. Shapoor pointed out to me that several of the homes were being built much like the one that we had built for ourselves the first year of our marriage. The fresh white plastered walls, the porches supported by tall poplar poles, the glass windows—these were great advances over the traditional one-room mud houses. We had never advised this kind of building, but since our home had been used as a community center everyone had seen it. Again I thought how much can be taught without even a word.

There were things in Sarbandan that saddened me. Both the girls' school and the boys' school were overcrowded and there were children who were not in school simply because there were not shoes enough in the village to go around. The clinic was still unsatisfactory and the government had done nothing about giving us a different doctor. But still more heartbreaking was the fact that our beautiful new factory stood idle. There were several reasons for this, but the most important seemed to be that there was no water available at the factory.

We had selected the site for the factory and CARE had built it with the thought that a well could be dug that would furnish the needed water. The well had been drilled down seventy feet but still there was no water. Experts decided that there was water available but the well would have to be deeper. While I was working in Dashte Moghan and visiting my family as frequently as I could, I spent much of my time in Teheran, working on the problem of this well. I applied to the Ministry of Health and received promises but no actual aid. I was told to apply to Teheran Austend (you would say in America Teheran County), which had a program of construction in which Point Four shared the expense and the people, themselves, gave half. Hours that I wanted to spend with my children and with my husband, I spent in sitting in government offices waiting for my turn for a brief interview. Perhaps the Agricultural Department could be of assistance here. But the Agricultural Department suggested that I try the Demavend Development Bongha. Always the answer was not a definite no, but a referral to some other department. It was impossible for me to understand this constant referral to a different agency. The Rish e safed, sitting in the teahouse of Mash'hadi Mokhtar, smoked and talked and smoked some more. "Who crosses the hand with silver? What hand?" one old man asked. From others I had heard the rumor that it was difficult to get cooperation for a project that could not bring pishkesh to someone.

The papers were filled with the work of Dr. Arsanjani, who was in charge of the land reform program. I determined while I was in Teheran that I would see him and tell him the long story of the village and the well.

When I called the office of Dr. Arsanjani to make an appointment I was told that he could be seen on Monday. Monday I was at the office when it opened. There I was treated with rudeness, perhaps because I am a woman. Four Mondays I spent in the office waiting for a consultation. Finally I was asked, "How much time will your business take?"

I held my temper. "How many minutes may I have? I will fit my story to the time that is given me."

"As few as possible," I was told.

Dr. Arsanjani received me with courtesy—it is only insignificant men who need the comfort of rudeness. "Tell me your story," he said. And so I told him the story of Sarbandan, of the progress of the people, of their dreams, of the factory, and of the well that was so needed. When I would have hurried he asked me to take my time. And when I had finished he said, "This sounds like a fairy story. I, myself, will visit this village." He did not say that his department would drive a well for us; but I was out of the office before I realized this.

I waited for him to call me, and after he had visited the village he did call and invited me for another interview. "This is the first time I have congratulated a woman," he said, "but I congratulate you. What you have done for this village is excellent. You should be working on a larger scale."

"Dashte Moghan?" I asked. I was eager to resume my work there and I couldn't understand why I had not been given a date for my return.

"I am not in charge there, of course," Dr. Arsanjani said, "but I understand that your appointment there is terminated."

I returned to Dashte Moghan to see that everything was in order and to leave Pooran to take my place; little Pooran, whose bent back had at first seemed an insurmountable obstacle in village work, had grown so capable that even the experienced specialists like Pahvine and Mrs. Hosseini were willing to work under her direction.

"I knew when you left us that you would never really return," Pooran said.

"You knew."

"You will always be moving; you will always be beginning for others to finish."

I put my arms around her. "Are you a prophet? Because if you are I am already tired of starting and going."

She laughed but there was a shakiness in her laughter. "Lady Najafi—Najmeh—as you have given to me, may God give to you."

I said good-bye to each of the villages. I gave my last word of advice. "Continue in the same pattern," I told my girls, looking with pride upon the things they, themselves, had done. "Repeat the pattern again and again and again."

"We will, Lady Najafi. May God keep you."

And so the farewell tray was arranged, covered with a white cloth. On it there were a flower, a small white Koran and a bowl of water in which one leaf floated. I approached the tray with my eyes dimmed with tears. I touched the flower. (Lay hold of beauty.) I kissed the Koran. (All beauty comes from God; God is the beginning and end of beauty.) and waited while Pahvine with her finger tips splashed some of the water from the bowl so that it fell upon me.

> *God keep you,*
> *God watch over you,*
> *God return you to us.*
> *You are never alone.*
> *We pray for you,*
> *May God go with you.*

Then Mrs. Hosseini held the Koran so that I could walk under it and the people followed me crying,

> *May God keep you,*
> *May God go with you.*

12 ❧ The Quake

"HOW MANY TIMES YOU CRY IN YOUR SLEEP, NAJMEH-JUN," SHA-poor said as we sat at breakfast.

Sina and Nassim looked at me with surprised eyes. "Don't cry, Mama," Nassim said. Mother, who was visiting us, put down her glass.

Abruptly the tears came to my eyes again and spilled down my cheeks. "I knew that I was dreaming always, dreaming that I cried. I did not know that I cried aloud."

"What is it? What . . . ?" Shapoor's voice was teasing.

"Many things." I went into the next room to wash my face.

"Sarbandan?" Shapoor asked, when I was again at the table.

Sarbandan was one thing. Again and again I had tried to get to the right people to get a well near the new factory. Again and again I had tried to get PLAN or some other department to furnish the raw material so that the looms might hum again. Still the factory wasn't working, though the girls had learned to operate the machines that now stood idle. The last time I had been in Sarbandan a piece of the corrugated iron roof that had come loose was flapping up and down in the wind. It had somehow seemed deeply sad to me that before the factory had even been used it was in need of repair.

"Sarbandan, perhaps," I answered Shapoor's question.

Abruptly his voice changed from affectionate teasing to a tone of sharpness. "I don't know what kind of woman you are, Najmeh. Don't you love your children? Sometime try crying about their long days with only Nannie and Ramazan."

I looked quickly at my mother, who had spent so many hours with the children, taking my place while I worked in the office. She said only, "My poor child. When I am gone who will understand her?"

In spite of what Shapoor had said about my leaving the children he knew and I knew that it was important that I hold a job and contribute to the support of the family. I was buying the home, for example, and without my salary where would we get the monthly payments? As soon as my contract in Dashte Moghan was terminated—and I still could not understand the reason for its termination—I applied at the offices of several governmental departments. Almost at once I was given a position in the office of the Minister of Agriculture. I certainly was not leaving the children because I wanted to. I don't like office work; I don't even enjoy administration. My life is working in the villages face to face, heart to heart with the women.

Yet, working in a government office I learned about how government offices are run. I found that those who make the most demands receive the most attention, which did not surprise me, but there were things I was not prepared for. One day into the office came a disreputable-looking middle-aged man who looked vaguely familiar to me.

"Who is he?" I asked an engineer in the office.

"He is a person of importance."

"In America there is a slang word for men who look like this. The word is 'hood.' "

"He has an appointment to see the Shah," the engineer told me. And then, "He is not to be laughed at in the world of sports or business."

"Why?" I asked.

He explained to me about the tie between politics and business. "Three banana boats come into the harbor. The people want bananas; they are hungry and bananas are good food. Why does the government allow only one to unload? I'll tell you. Then the price of bananas is high."

"This is rumor. Not fact," I declared.

He nodded. "It is rumor, yes. But where is rumor born except from the womb of fact?"

Dimly I began to see the walls that enclose the Shah, all of the excellent ministers of the government, everybody who would bring Iran abreast of the modern world.

So perhaps my crying was for the unfinished women's programs as well as for Sarbandan.

The deeper government problems I could do nothing about; but perhaps I could start the looms in Sarbandan. I turned again to CARE. At CARE there was a new assistant director, Mr. Davis. I liked him at once and he was interested in the silent factory at Sarbandan. Mr. Davis and I went together to the city of Shalus, where there are spinning machines brought to Iran by Reza Shah. Here I met a Mr. Fotoohe, a textile designer. We would run the factory without a well, I decided. Every worker could come bringing her jug of water for tea. For the treatment of materials, for the aftabe, the water could be brought by donkey. Mr. Fotoohe knew what textiles could best be produced on our looms. He also knew what materials could most readily be sold in Iran or in the export markets. We talked together for many hours and Mr. Fotoohe made a plan for me to present to the government.

I presented the plan and Dr. Arsanjani stopped at my desk one day, the plan in his hand. "Did you know that the cooperative in Sarbandan is not correctly registered?"

I didn't answer. I simply put my head on my arms folded on my desk. Twenty bus trips to Sarbandan later the registration was approved. Now we waited for the right government department to review the plans for the factory.

This was the summer of my greatest discouragement. Evenings as I sat on the floor with the children, with my mouth I talked with them about their own small happinesses, but with my heart I said, "Najmeh, why aren't you like other women? Why can't you be content as Fakhri is content?"

Shapoor had brought a little model sports car from America as a gift for Sina. It was the sort of car with a million pieces that an

American teen-ager who knew the inside of a big car would enjoy assembling. I sat with the complex directions before me, the glue tube in my hand and the children examining and breaking up the minute parts before I could put them together. And I thought, *My life is like this. The parts should go together neatly like a child's puzzle. Instead it is like this car. All of the pieces fit somewhere, but who knows where?*

It was almost eleven on a clear September night. The children were in bed but Shapoor and I were sitting in our garden by the pool enjoying the evening breeze. Summer days may be warm in Teheran, but the evenings are usually cool, and in Teheran September is still summer. With my head thrown back I was counting the constellations that I knew by name.

Abruptly I forgot the stars. The earth shook under me. I wondered for a moment if I were ill and the feeling of movement was some sort of hallucination, but I looked into our pool and the water was still sloshing back and forth against the sides.

"An earthquake?" I asked Shapoor.

Again the earth shook, and I hurried into the house, followed by Shapoor, to see if the children were all right. They had been rolled from side to side in their beds but neither had awakened. Sina, more nervous than Nassim, was whimpering a little in his sleep. I wiped the moisture from his forehead, stooped and kissed him, then turned to Shapoor.

"I must go," I said.

"Go where?" he asked.

"Where I am needed."

"Najmeh, you are a mother. You are needed here."

I had been lounging in pajamas and a robe. Now I began to dress.

"Look," Shapoor said reasonably, "you don't even know where this earthquake is. It may be a hundred miles from here."

"It is in Iran," I said. "That is enough for me."

"I'm not about to start off to hunt a partridge somewhere in the brush," Shapoor said.

"I know. Take me to Mohsen. That's all I want you to do."

He began to lace up his shoes and I went to ask Ramazan to waken and stay up to comfort the children until their father returned.

At Mohsen's house the lights were on and Mohsen was dressed and walking back and forth through his living rooms. He didn't seem surprised to see me. "I have found a little information though we can't get much until morning, I imagine. The earthquake is about ninety or a hundred miles from here."

"In which direction?"

"The Kazvin area."

He took a rolled map from behind the books in a glass-doored bookcase. He unrolled it and we studied it together. "Here is Buin." He put his finger on a point of the map. "The quake must have been somewhere there."

I ran my finger over the area. It is a rugged mountain section. "There must be a hundred villages or more," I said. And Mohsen added, "At least a hundred. I have been often there. Many villages are not even reached by roads."

I had forgotten that Shapoor was waiting for me. I went to him and put my cheek against his hand. "Please understand. Please. I must go."

He ran his fingers up through my hair from the back of my neck to the crown of my head but he did not take my hand or offer to kiss me.

"Mother will take care of my home."

Mohsen went to speak to Mother. She was already dressed and was wrapping herself in her black chadar. "My poor child," she said as she kissed me and left with Shapoor.

"CARE will be there. The Red Lion and Sun. The—" Mohsen began.

"Mohsen, we are not going to Buin. I think the Shah will go there. We won't go to Dapisfahen. The Red Lion and Sun will reach these cities. Mohsen, let's go to the villages, the small ones where others may not think to go. You know this country and I know the common people and how they act in disaster."

"We cannot go empty-handed. It is better to go more slowly and go with a filled basket."

Mohsen sat at his telephone. Although there had been aftershocks the lines weren't down but the switchboards were crowded. Finally he reached three other businessmen who had trucks, and he arranged to have them meet him soon at his place of business in the bazaar.

Mohsen lifted me onto the high seat of his truck and got in under the wheel. "Sister, make a list of things most needed."

"Water comes first."

"The qanats will be destroyed if the quake is as disastrous as the first reports say."

"Water, bread, kerosene, matches . . ."

I stopped talking. The streets of Teheran were filled with people, not moving around, not speaking with each other. Groups were sitting motionless on the streets and drivers of vehicles like ours had to avoid the people because the people were too horror-stricken to move out of the way.

"Water, bread, kerosene, matches, blankets, shrouds . . ."

At the bazaar were two trucks. The third friend had not yet arrived. Although morning was beginning to gray, our headlights attracted a crowd.

"We are going to the earthquake," Mohsen said.

"If you are going, take this." One man hurried to his booth in the bazaar and came back with an armload of blankets, which he steadied with his chin to keep them from falling.

"Can you afford—?" Mohsen began, but the man said, "He who has one blanket is rich when others are without blankets."

Soon the trucks began filling with bread and rice and blankets. I asked for jars and pots and soon we were filling these with clear fresh Teheran water and arranging them so that the water would not be spilled. Some gave money, urging it into our hands. "If you are going, take this." We had two tents. Kerosene, candles, matches, and . . . shrouds.

With the money in my hand I bought tea and sugar and dates. I bought pipes and tobacco for the aged. And fruits and biscuits.

It was morning before the three trucks were loaded and we were on our way to the Kazvin area. Still we did not know just what had happened, but word was coming in that everyone had been crushed by the collapse of their houses. Seventy miles out of Teheran we began to see stragglers on the road, moving like sleepwalkers away from the ruin that had once been their world.

Larger trucks passed us. Mr. Sakalis of CARE saluted me as his truck passed ours.

Mohsen and his friends had agreed that our trucks would stay as close together as possible so that we could carry out some kind of program to make our materials serve the most people.

The first village at which Mohsen and I stopped was a village of the dead. "Come, Sister." Mohsen lifted me from the truck and took my hand to help me over the deeply scarred earth. Together, wordless, we walked toward the earthquake-broken wall of a small village. We stopped a moment and listened for the wailing that accompanies death in my country. We heard, or thought we heard, the movement of big black wings as vultures circled over the village.

"Come, Sister," Mohsen said again. I put my scarf over my nose and mouth in a useless attempt to close out the stench of death. We waited a few feet from the wall. Still we heard no human sound. Mohsen gestured toward the truck filled with water, bread, tea, sugar, kerosene, matches, blankets, shrouds for the burial of the dead. "There is no one living to use these things." Mohsen's voice was scarcely more than a whisper. Together we walked all the way around the wall looking for an opening. There might yet be something we could do. There had been but one entrance to the wall and that had been completely closed by a fall of bricks, probably at the first shock. There had been no way of escape from the village. The heavy dome-shaped roofs of the mud houses had fallen upon the sleeping people. If any had escaped this fate the closed wall had prevented him from coming out into the open country before the later shocks.

We turned back to the truck and Mohsen lifted me onto the high seat. Sometime the soldiers would come with their masked faces and shovels to enter the village, clear away the rubble and put quick lime upon the bodies the vultures had not devoured. I saw tears standing in Mohsen's eyes, but I was still too horrified to weep.

We were in the truck before he said, "Najmeh-jun, the people who built these walls to save themselves built their own tomb." I looked at Mohsen, and I thought, *Brother, you said a wise thing. Who can build a wall without walling in the seeds of death and decay and walling out all other things?*

"This is a parable," I told him. "Once there was a great people who were brave and strong and spread themselves over the face of the known world, carrying with them music, literature, art, justice and the worship of one God. But time turned and turned again and the men's hearts grew smaller. Now they no longer spread themselves into other lands. They stopped where they were and built walls. They built walls of masonry to keep out the sand, the robber, the invading armies. They built walls of fear and ignorance and superstition to keep out new developments, new philosophies."

Then I was silent for a time and we both listened to the laboring of the truck's engine and steadied ourselves with difficulty against the jolts in the destroyed road. Finally Mohsen said, "What is the end of this fable? Did an earthquake destroy these people?"

"I do not want an earthquake in my story. I want a happier ending. Yet something must destroy the walls."

Again we were without words, but finally I said, "And then one day came a wind. It was not a tornado. Rather it was a first small zephyr that later grew to be a persuasive breeze. This wind blew with persistence against the walls but the walls resisted the pressure. Finally the wind circled around and around the walls until it found a slight break. Through this fissure it blew its breath until the break grew larger and larger and finally the wall crumbled and disappeared. Now this did not happen all at once, but grain of sand by grain of sand. Sometimes the breeze found a large opening, a gate perhaps that had been left open especially for it, and then it carried its breath into the city in spite of the walls."

"And then?" Mohsen asked. "Is that the end of the fable?"

"I don't know. I wish that I did know."

"And are you the wind, Najmeh-jun?"

"I am part of the wind. A very small part."

"And you have found a fissure in the wall, Sister?"

"Some crevices, perhaps. But even as I have found these crevices I have discovered that the walls are heavier, more formidable than I dreamed of. They are built not only of ignorance and fear and superstition—but of the pain of others."

And there in the distance were the tumbled walls of another village.

As we drew near we discovered that only about three-fourths of the houses had been crumpled. The living were shocked into immobility. No words came from the mouths. "First we must find the mullah of this village if he still lives," I told Mohsen and Mohsen went to search for him. Shortly he came back with the old man, who was twisting his hands and crying, "Wherein have we sinned that God should settle his wrath upon us? Wherein have we sinned?"

I spoke sternly to him. I was the father and he the child. "Father," I said, "it is for you to lift up your heart. To stand there wailing now is indeed a sin. Help us to find those in need of water and food so that we can give it to them."

"Water? Food?" He still twisted his hands together. But he went away and in a moment there came a file of wounded and hungry from the village. We had set up one of our tents as a first-aid center and I was trying to give the aid. One woman brought a child with a broken leg. A white bone protruded from the child's calf. "This boy is broken," the mother wailed. "You must put him in your truck and take him to a doctor."

"There is no doctor."

"In Teheran," the mother insisted. "This boy is broken."

I took the child's foot. As I jerked the leg straight he screamed, but the bone disappeared inside the leg and I was able to medicate and bandage the wound. "He must not walk," I said.

"You are not any more human," the mother accused me.

How could I make her understand that our trucks must be used to distribute supplies? That one child's leg could not delay the saving of many lives.

With supplies distributed in the first village—water, food, blankets and shrouds—we moved on to another village and set up our second tent. Already one of the trucks had returned to Teheran. In this village the Mullah waited for us. He was a young man with a face yellow-gray from fatigue. "We prayed someone would find us," he said. "Give me work to do."

Then came a young woman with long black hair matted and torn, her face a mask of agony. "I have lost my shoes," she cried. "No one will help me find my beautiful new shoes."

The Mullah spoke close to my ear. "She was to have been married tomorrow. She just now saw her crushed fiancé removed from a crumbled house. Her parents are gone too and she is the only one left."

"Here is hot tea," I said, offering her a glass, but she pushed it away with the back of her hand. "No one will help me find my wedding shoes," she cried.

"She misses her mind," the Mullah said with tenderness.

I offered him the glass of tea and he took it gratefully. "I almost feel as if I am missing mine," he said.

"You have a piece of your heart in your mind," I told him, loving all of the mullahs of Islam who, like this man, are servants of the poor.

For three nights and days we worked in the earthquake area. With two tents, three trucks, twelve men to take the seriously injured— perhaps the dying—to the hospitals and to bring back more supplies for relief, six men taking shovels to help with the burials, and two to give out the shrouds and water for the washing of the dead. The Mullah himself supervised the work of the villagers in digging through the rubble for bodies.

As we moved our relief supplies to a third village, whole groups of hungry stragglers met us on the road with their hands pulling at their lower lips in the universal sign of hunger. For these we left food and blankets.

Three days and nights and we had reached only three villages. This was not a drop of water in an ocean. More than a hundred villages had been destroyed. Fifty out of ninety inhabitants had died. The fault thirty miles beneath the surface was sixty miles long and twenty-five miles wide. In the city of Buin 3,000 of the 6,000 people had died in one horrifying minute. When the Shah had arrived in Buin the grimy, sobbing villagers had met him. One old woman had thrown herself at his feet and cried, "I have lost all I had, O Father of the Nation. My husband, my two sons, four daughters, two brothers and their nine children."

In Danesfahen, where 4,500 people lived, 3,200 perished. This was the epicenter of the quake.

And as we worked in the villages we said to each other, "If this quake had been ninety miles from here, if it had struck with all of its force in Teheran, one million would have died."

In some of the remote villages where supplies and help had to be taken in by donkey the people huddled in the ruins of their villages without food or water for three or four days.

But in spite of the sleepwalking horror of these nights and days there were some heartening things. Help came from all over the world, from Finland to New Zealand. Within twenty-eight hours from the time of the first shock, an American hospital, housed in tents and manned by doctors and nurses, had arrived by air from West Germany.

Calamity is a big stick that stirs the hearts of everyone.

And when I returned home I could not believe that Shapoor was interested in a crack in our garden wall, opened with that first shock on that quiet, starry September evening.

13 ❧ My American Family

I STRUGGLED TO EMERGE FROM A STRANGE DREAM. I HAD BEEN swimming, fighting against wave after wave that swept over me. At last, the sand sucking at my feet, I had staggered to the beach and lay out of reach of the sea on the safe hot sand. The sun was there, the sand, the blue sky, but nothing else, and I wondered where I was and how I had escaped drowning in the persistent surging of the water. Then I felt that I dreamed but I couldn't awaken. Finally Nassim cried out and I arose to take her a drink and to soothe her.

When I returned to bed I lay quietly trying to interpret the dream. The meaning evaded me and it was gray morning before I realized what it meant—at least to me. My marriage was like the sea. The happiness, the lightness, the joy were gone from it. In a strange subconscious way I had been fighting against the restrictions that marriage imposes, against the breaking up of myself by its ceaseless assault on all that was deeply me. I wondered how, when, this had happened to Shapoor and me. Was it the result of the constantly reiterated criticism from Shapoor's family that I did not care for him deeply enough to make a good wife. Perhaps it was his annoyance with me when I left the children to assist those who suffered from the earthquake and his preoccupation with the small crack in the wall of our garden when I had tried to tell him of the disaster area. Or was it when I learned that he had insisted on my being dismissed from my position in Dashte Moghan so that I could take an office position—a position which offered no challenge to me—in Teheran.

Or—and the thought startled me—perhaps it was on our wedding night when I had left our bed to go to the aid of a man injured in a knife fight. Perhaps our marriage had never been right.

I fell asleep after the sun had risen, but when it was time to get up and hurry to get to our separate offices I felt entirely unable to cope with life. The children felt my mood and dallied instead of cooperating, and when Shapoor treated them with roughness—in the Persian manner of father to child—my anger broke from me.

"You must leave this house," I told him.

He replied, "This is my home. If it cannot shelter both of us perhaps you should go. Again."

I might have said, "But I selected and furnished this home. With my own money—" But I didn't. The memory of the battle to reach the warm sunny sand, away from the pummeling of the sea felt only in my dream, prompted me to say, "I'll go."

My mother, always quick to understand, looked at me sorrowfully when I told her of this break, but she consented to come to my home and take my place with the children and keep Shapoor in comfort. I didn't think of my going as a separation, as a divorce. I thought of being alone to find myself in the ruins of my plans. I didn't want sympathy and even less did I want to hear, "I told you so." I would not go to any member of my family. Sarbandan, ninety kilometers from Teheran, was too far away from my office for me to stay in the village. Besides, the house that Shapoor and I had built together would confuse me with warm memories of the plans we had made.

I took a small apartment not too far from my office, but I did not stay there long. A cold that had been deepening even before I had been immersed in this strange dream now grew abruptly worse. I called at a doctor's office. "How can you be walking around?" he inquired. "To the hospital with you. You have pneumonia."

So I went to the hospital, not caring too much for life, except that the factory in Sarbandan was standing idle and my hundreds of letters to different departments hadn't as yet brought me any response. Except that Nassim and Sina were asking Mother when I was coming home and crying for me.

My sisters and brothers came to see me. So did my nephews Ali and Amir. When they came into Teheran my girls who had worked with me in Sarbandan, in Baluchistan, in Dashte Moghan brought flowers and told me of their developing projects. But Shapoor did not come. I heard that he was spending most of his time with his family but that he had some hours for card playing and he knew how I hated gambling.

It was then that I thought about the possibility of legal separation, of divorce. I mentioned this to one of my brothers and he said, "Najmeh-jun, you know the law in Iran. The children always go to the father unless the court finds him unfit and unworthy or unless he formally consents to the wife's having the children. Shapoor is a good man, a good father. He loves his children and his mother would gladly take care of them."

"I know," I agreed. "I know all that and I won't give up my children." I thought longingly of the warm, quiet sand away from the reach of the pummeling waves. "Yes, I know all that."

I was lying on my bed considering the difference between my dreams and reality when I received a letter from my American family. Ma'am and Daddy Jones and their daughter, Sammie, would be in Teheran for No Ruz.

Immediately I was nudged from the nest of self-pity I had been brooding on. My American family, in Teheran! They loved Shapoor as they loved me. Why should they come halfway around the world to find our home broken? Who would show them the wonders of Iran if we did not? I must arrange a temporary reconciliation. I must return to my home, and when the plane brought these people we loved so much into the Teheran airport we must both be there, standing together, to greet them.

I wondered if Shapoor would be reluctant to cooperate; but he was not only willing but happy to make plans with me. Back in our little home we both tried hard to act as if the bitter break had not occurred. The children must not be allowed to feel any strain between us. I went back to a job at the office of PLAN and Shapoor was working, but there was still much to be done at home. The children must be moved into our room with us and three single cots set up in the double room the children occupied. Ma'am enjoyed a tub bath, not a shower, so we purchased an enameled bathtub. A tap was arranged so that water could flow into the tub. No one knew much about such plumbing, so when the plug was released the water ran over the floor and out the drain that carried the water from the shower. I should have liked to replace the floor latrine with a Western water closet but that would have taken both time and money, neither of which we had.

There must be flowers in every room, American food in the refrigerator, Mother in my home to greet my guests. I forgot that I had been ill and Shapoor and I both almost forgot that we had been angry.

The evening of the family's arrival we drove the Volkswagen to the airport; my nephew Ali drove his father's large car. We parked swiftly and lined up with the pushing crowd before the large glass windows.

"There they are," I cried, and Ali asked, "Where? Where?"

"There."

Ma'am, pink-faced and shining, Daddy unchanged, and Sammie, who had been a child six years before, now a young lady slender and so tall that she could look down upon the heads of the Persian officials who were scrutinizing the contents of her suitcase.

"They see us," Shapoor cried, gesturing wildly.

"They do see us." I waved, too, feeling in a strange unexplainable way that my two separate lives—American and Persian—were about to be fused.

When at last they had gone through customs and were allowed to come outside to us, we embraced with tears. Daddy went with Shapoor in the Volks; Ali, Sammie, Ma'am and I in the big car with all the luggage.

With love Ma'am greeted Mother, though both were wordless except for "Salaam." She exclaimed over the beauty of our salon, and we all talked at once about everything—about everything but the dark thing that lay between Shapoor and me.

It was not until later that I learned that Daddy, blunt but loving, had inquired of Shapoor about the separation of which they had heard rumors. Shapoor had told Daddy that he loved me and wanted me. That he wished our break to end. He had been influenced by his family, which felt that he, their eldest son, deserved a full-time wife.

Daddy had tentatively put forward the idea that a part of a specially good wife might be better than all of an ordinary woman. I imagine that they both laughed, since Daddy has part of a good wife.

For once in my adult life I wished that I were like Fahkri or Fahti, sitting in my home with nothing to do but be a lady; there was so much I wanted to do for my guests, there were so many things that I wanted them to see, so many people I wanted them to know. So much I wanted to discuss with Ma'am, the two of us alone together.

As soon as I spoke to others of their coming many were eager to entertain my California family. All of my brothers and sisters; Shapoor's family; my nephew Amir, who had been a son in the Jones family for three years; the families of other Iranian students studying in California.

"We must take our vacations," I had told Shapoor as we had planned for the family's arrival.

"If we can," he agreed. "We want to take them south to Shiraz, Persepolis, Isfahan, Ghom."

"And to the Caspian," I added. "And to Sarbandan."

Shapoor was able to get only three days at No Ruz so I went south with the family and Shapoor arranged to join us in Shiraz for the No Ruz vacation.

The dun-colored world stretched away to low sand hills on both sides of the road as we traveled south by bus. Ma'am had insisted on taking the bus to get closer to the country. Occasionally far from the road we saw the green of irrigated fields and I pointed out the great saucerlike circles of sand that mark the course of the qanats, our underground irrigation canals. Standing in line, men and women together, to use an outdoor latrine, Sammie made friends with the women. In queues in my country the men go ahead of the women. This, of course, was new to Sammie and she pantomimed the hustling by of the men much to the delight of the women. When we again boarded the bus the women had accepted the Americans completely and one of them poured almonds from a kerosene can onto our laps.

Even with the diversion of cracking and eating, talking and dozing, sixteen hours on an ancient bus is very long. When we reached Shiraz we were through with bus travel!

Later Ma'am and I left Daddy and Sammie in Shiraz and took a two-engine plane to Bushire on the Gulf Coast. For the first time the two of us together had leisure and quiet to probe for the answers my life seemed to lack. My mother had always understood me, she had supported me in anything I wished to do, but she was not in close enough touch with the modern world to counsel me. How do American women conduct their double lives, I wanted to know. In Iran it is more difficult, Ma'am agreed, but still not impossible for a woman to make two lives productive. When I was married, I told her, I was expected to be a painted doll spending my time in visiting and being visited, in arranging flowers, in pouring tea, in managing servants, keeping the home beautiful. In America more and more young women prepare for the professions, expecting to work until their husbands are launched in careers or even longer if they find they have deep interests or unusual capabilities. But when they find their interests are divergent from those of their husbands, what then? Or if the work of the woman overshadows that of the man? Divorce is possible, of course, but if there is love, if there are children, there must be other answers.

Just as I was beginning to find peace in Ma'am's tranquillity as we walked through the almost deserted city or rested in the home of the director of CARE in the area, an engineer with whom I had worked in Baluchistan invited us to ride with him. He wanted us to see the progress of an agricultural project in a burned-up famine-ridden land, and to watch the sun set over the sea. Asking Ma'am to forgive our speaking in Farsi, we talked about the situation of educated young people in any developing country, young people, especially, who had studied in America. We discussed the difficulty of putting what we learned in America behind us and trying to fit into the traditional pattern—the pattern that is expected of us, especially of the women. He told me in an impassioned voice that neither I nor his wife, a medical doctor, should have married. Women who wish to serve in the professions should not divide their loyalties between those they serve and their own husband and children. "Leave Iran," he begged me. "Return to the United States and pursue your writing career." I listened to his words. I knew what he was talking about. We had shared many of the same frustrations in trying to help our people to advance five hundred years, from serfdom to responsible government, all in one generation. We had pushed against the same closed doors until our spirits were bruised and broken, and yet in this I had already studied my heart and knew my own answers. "I will never desert my people," I told him. "Never."

Was he right about professional women's having no place in marriage? It shook me that this advanced engineer who had spent many years in America felt about his wife's profession as Shapoor felt about mine. But when I had declared that I would "never desert my people. Never," I had meant that not only the lure of America but the lure of a tranquil household would not take me from my work.

When we returned to Shiraz I was deeply troubled, but I tried to put my brooding away for a later day because Shapoor arrived full of life and gaiety and it was time for us to be tourists.

The most important places to go in this beautiful city of roses are the tombs of two of the greatest Persian poets, Hafiz and Saudi. I had always preferred the poems of Hafiz, but this time it was the tomb of Saudi that spoke to me in a very special way.

Above the tomb of Saudi there is a beautiful mosaic panel, one of the most beautiful panels in the world. On it is pictured with infinite skill the willow motif that is often used in Iranian decoration. Because my country is so largely desert, the tree, especially the willow tree, has special significance. Three willow trees grow close together, as birches are planted in America. The three slender silver trunks seem to grow out of the same bit of soil; each rises independently but in graceful relation to the others, and from the trunks grow intertwined branches that form one lacy shade.

"There you are, Najmeh," Ma'am said and she needed to say no more. The three slender trunks—Najmeh, herself; Najmeh, the administrator, organizer, social worker; and Najmeh, wife and mother; all three growing equally but in relation to each other and forming one shade.

"I understand," I said, feeling the beauty of the mosaic holding my heart.

Later, in our hotel room in Isfahan with no interruptions by the children, no family or servant crisis to be taken care of, no unexpected telephone calls, I said, "Shapoor, we must talk."

He sat on the floor, his back against the bed, and I dropped down beside him though I saw a spider scurry across the floor and disappear into the shower room. I had thought that I would speak of the three willows that are really one, but the words were not easy to me. Instead I simply said, "Let's try again, Shapoor."

He ruffled my hair in the playful, gentle way he has. "I will try, Najmeh. Without you nothing was right."

Communication was not easy between us because we each hesitated to break the spirit we had recaptured; but we talked of my work. I was eager to get operations started at the factory. He would help in every way that he could, he promised. I hated office work and would like to get again into the field. He understood.

When the five of us returned to Teheran we stopped briefly in Ghom, one of the religious centers of my country. Shapoor went into the mosque but I did not. Still my resolution to be complete in the way the willow tree motif is complete became to me almost a religious dedication.

But when, back in Teheran, I put on my black dress, my traditional black chadar, and attended the woman's gathering at the funeral of an aged relative of Shapoor—a person whom I had loved and respected—and went around the circle of mourners offering my hand to each, Shapoor's sister and his mother turned their faces away from my offered hand.

The future would be difficult for Shapoor—and for me.

14 ❧ The Heart of CARE

FARVARDIN, APRIL, IN SARBANDAN WITH THE FILM OF APRICOT AND cherry blossoms sifting through the air on the soft spring breeze. Although the trees against the incredibly blue sky are still delicately white and pink, the green-carpeted earth beneath them is delicately drifted with petals. Through the lanes of the village men drive their donkeys, laden with packs of soil to renew old fields, or clay bricks to rebuild fallen walls. A herd of sheep, on its way to the upper pastures, fills the main street from wall to wall and I smile as I see a disgusted housewife, unable to push through the sheep to reach the jube, throw down the water bucket she is carrying.

Children are everywhere, though they should be in school, the little girls with babies jouncing on their backs as they toss a pebble and hop through an intricate pattern to pick it up. Three old men sit in the shade of the teahouse of Mash'hadi Mokhtar drinking tea and continuing an endless discussion of national affairs. Five young men are gathered around the front of the bus. Mahrubi, the young brother of Mash'hadi Mokhtar, has the hood up and is making what seems to these youths to be a major manipulation.

It is spring, the village is beautiful and alive, and I am glad that Ma'am and Daddy and Sammie will see my village at its best.

I had come from Sarbandan the day before to see that everything was in readiness for the visit. When the family got off the bus a hundred curious eyes were upon them but few people were on the street. "Don't take pictures of the people without first asking them," I told Daddy. "Especially the women."

We went first to my home. This would be much more than just

167

another house to my American family because they knew the story of the building. Next we visited the girls' school. One of the small scholars had been excused from her lessons to tend the baby of the teacher. I must look into this. The boys' school was not open to us because the young principal distrusted me and feared that I would interfere with his methods. Ma'am, Sammie and I walked through the bathhouse. The women, sitting naked in the pleasant steam, went on washing their little brown babies. We made a wide circle around the clinic with its broken wall, its fetid odor.

And finally there was the factory; the beautiful new building with *CARE, a Gift from the People of the United States* printed on it in both Farsi and English. We looked inside at the sixteen quiet looms. Outside again Ma'am's eyes filled with tears when she saw the piece of the corrugated roof flapping in the breeze.

For Ma'am, for everyone who had faith in me, I must do something to put this factory in operation!

Many of the people of the village were eager to entertain my guests. We went from the home of the tall Kadkhoda, to the home of Ramazan's parents, to the home of Mash'hadi Mokhtar. In every home we sat together upon the carpet and drank tea, and ate dried watermelon seeds, shelled apricot seeds, dried apricots and cherries and cookies, a luxury purchased for this great occasion. With me everywhere went Asghar, the wonderful boy who had been my servant when I first came to Sarbandan and who was now married with a family of his own. How I wished that Ma'am could speak the language of these people as easily as she read their hearts.

Later, as we watched the sun set over the western field, she asked questions and questions about the improvements in the village. What must one do, what preparations must one make so that improvements built at a great sacrifice can be self-perpetuating? Must the change be made in the people themselves? And how can this be done? But Sammie said, "I can't stand to see any more patches. There is an old saying in America, 'Patch beside patch is economy; but patch upon patch is poverty.' "

"You have American eyes," I told Sammie gently. "In the villages of Iran people are fortunate to have garments to patch."

"But the barefooted men and women!" she protested.

"Shoes are not necessary in the summer." I did not say that for many they are not available in the winter.

"Can't we send shoes and clothing?" Sammie asked.

"Our government charges import duty on even used clothes," I told her. "And besides clothing wears out. There is one way to help these people and that is to give them a way to earn these necessities for themselves."

"And so," Ma'am said, "we are right back to the factory."

"We are right back at the factory," I agreed.

For six weeks my American family stayed in Iran. Shapoor and I took them over the naked Elburz Mountains to the Caspian Sea. They responded to the overpowering grandeur of the almost un-scalable rock mountains as the Volkswagen climbed the German-engineered highway that loops back and forth until sixteen levels of the same road can be seen from a point near the summit. They responded in a different way to the quiet green of the tea gardens in the warm lowland of the Caspian area. There women, dressed in bright-colored clothing, bend over the low bushes, and in the rice paddies the women, up to their knees in water, work shoulder to shoulder with their men.

"How hard the woman's life is," Sammie said.

But I thought, How simple. These women are expected to be people as well as women. Their ambition is to feed, clothe, and shelter their children, and the means to do these things are right here in the fields.

Abruptly the six weeks were ended. No more would Sammie set Ramazan's poor devoted heart to racing as she played ball with Nassim and Sina in the courtyard and contrary to Persian custom asked him to join in the game; no more would Daddy explore Teheran in his quiet, independent way; no more would Ma'am and I, sharing one heart between us, talk of Najmeh and the three willow trees that grow to make one perfect shade.

We were all tearful at the airport when Shapoor and his family, I and mine, and the other friends of the Jones family met to say good-bye. "Is this a haji?" one of my friends laughingly asked as he passed us in the waiting room. So many people! We might all have been going on a religious pilgrimage to Mecca! I felt that I couldn't let this experience end, yet in my heart I was happier than I had been for a long time. This was to have been the end of the reconciliation between Shapoor and me, but he had been helpful and gentle, the children had been so happy to have us both at home. The long conversations between Ma'am and me had helped me to be objective about our problems, and, after all, Shapoor had told Daddy that he loved and wanted me.

I had missed many days at the office so now I hurried to demolish the pile of work that had built up in my absence. I was supposed to direct research into the results that PLAN was getting from its expenditure of money, particularly in the field of education. Now my department head told me, "You are a wonderful woman, and I respect you for the good things you have done, but you are a terrible office worker." We both laughed but I knew that he meant what he said. In order to spend more time with Ma'am I had not risked having the office say "no" to a request for a few days off to take an important trip so I had simply stayed away. I must now prove that such behavior was exceptional not habitual. I was eager to check on many things in Sarbandan but first I must catch up with the work in my office. I almost hated the routine tasks that kept me in Teheran; but it was my work and I pushed determinedly through it.

One day Musi, bringing the bus to Teheran, called my home and left a message. The doctor had left the clinic and Mash'hadi Mokhtar wanted me to come at once.

For months—even years—I had been urging that the doctor who had ruined our clinic should leave Sarbandan. The Health Department had promised time after time to investigate but nothing had ever been done. I had talked to the doctor myself, urging him to build himself a house, improve his services or leave. Now he had gone.

Thursday afternoon as I left my office, Shapoor called for me and we drove to Sarbandan. I stopped first at the teahouse and Mash'hadi

Mokhtar's young brother Malek came hurrying to tell me the news. That morning the neighbors had heard no sound from the clinic. No sounds with a wife, an ancient mother, eleven daughters and one son! Little Rabbit, the son of the tall Kadkhoda, bolder than the other children, had investigated. The door was standing open but the family had left in the night.

Next we went to the clinic and looked in. Filth, refuse, but no people. Immediately we organized work groups. The women swept, scrubbed, scoured. The men mended the crumbling wall and applied new whitewash. I took inventory of equipment and supplies— almost nothing of value had been left—and made a list of materials we would need to reopen the clinic to care for the people who had built it. There was a festive spirit in the work, laughter and banter and gaiety I had missed in the village for some time.

As soon as the clinic smelled of whitewash and disinfectant instead of urine and human excrement, I notified the Health Department that the doctor had left, sneaked away, and the clinic was prepared for a new doctor. Had the doctor been threatened? Was he afraid of physical harm? Who knows?

Within ten days a new doctor had arrived in the village. All of the people had hoped that their first trusted doctor would return, but he and his courageous wife had chosen to go to Bandar Abbas, where conditions were much as I had found them in Baluchistan. Because they are devoted, dedicated people they had chosen the most difficult assignment open to them. Again Musi, bringing the bus to Teheran, left word for me to come to Sarbandan and Shapoor and I hurried to the village. I sat in the shining clean waiting room and discussed with the doctor the feeling that the people had for the clinic since they had built it themselves. He was a middle-aged man with both strength and compassion. He had been told that I would outline his responsibilities.

"This clinic does not serve Sarbandan only? No?" he asked.

"Where in Iran is there a doctor for sixteen hundred people? Sarbandan is the center for several mountain villages: Roodehan, Sargorg, Ah Sadat, Mahalah, Khosravan, Japon. Japon has a clinic but it is not open every day. We are fortunate to have a doctor for eight thousand people."

The doctor smiled. "It is good that mountain people are healthy —that all are not sick at one time."

Then I told him of Madar-i-Kadkhoda, who still brought the babies; of the women who still prepared magic potions for their little ones; of the old men who had some man who could write, prepare a prayer, really a magic charm, to prevent illness.

But I also told him of the success we had had with our inoculation and vaccination programs; of the efforts of the mothers to cooperate in our attempts to improve the sanitary conditions, purify the water, learn more of child care.

"I shall enjoy Sarbandan," he said. "Already I have employed masons to build me a home."

Only the young men of the village missed the laughing daughters of the man who had packed them up and flown.

Once the grocer's son, much in love with one of the doctor's daughters, had climbed through a window to pay court to her. In the darkness the other sisters had thought the noise he had made was caused by a robber, so they had all fallen upon him and beaten him before they threw him out. After that he had been shamed in the village. Perhaps now that the sisters had been taken away he would again dare to show his face.

There was so much to check on in Sarbandan that Shapoor and I established a regular routine of visits. Each Thursday evening he called for me at the office. Since there was never any packing to do— we kept village clothing and extra toilet articles in our Sarbandan home—we could go directly to the village.

One Thursday evening we were not out of our car before Mash'hadi Mokhtar sent his young brother, Malek, to tell me that the council was eager to hold a meeting. "Come to this home," I said. "We shall eat and then we shall discuss these problems."

Though both Kutchiki, the short Kadkhoda, and Mohradi, the tall Kadkhoda, were there, Mash'hadi Mokhtar was the voice of the group. Whenever there was anything unpleasant to say he was chosen to say it. Perhaps because he seemed to enjoy bad news.

"Lady Najafi," he said with few preliminaries and before the hubbly-bubblies were making soft music in the room, "we are not satisfied."

I waited for him to continue.

"You asked us to give land and labor for the clinic. For a longer time than we want to count it was filthy and useless. It was better to have died clean than to enter that place."

"This is of the past," I told him. "The clinic is now clean and the doctor is kind and efficient." I might have mentioned the hundreds of times I had spent my lunch hour waiting in offices to see officials who could remove the incompetent doctor, only to be told to see someone else. I waited silently, looking at the dark faces set in sharp relief by the lantern light. Surely Mash'hadi Mokhtar had not wanted this meeting to discuss a problem that was already solved.

In a few moments he went on: "You asked us to give land for a factory. We gave the land. With our hands we built the wall. Now in the factory nothing happens. Our wives and daughters hurried to the factory to learn to weave. We thought the factory was the best thing that had ever happened to Sarbandan. But it is nothing."

What could I say? That I had been promised by PLAN that we would receive financial help? That there had been four changes of prime ministers since the original agreement had been made? That the Ministry of Court, the Ministry of Industry, the Institute of Textiles, the Agricultural Bank and the Industrial Development Bank had all promised help but had been unable to carry out their promises? That I had broken my heart against the lack of concern in government departments? That I was more disappointed than the men of the village?

"There is still CARE," I said. "But the policies are formulated in America."

"They might as well be formulated in Paradise," Mash'hadi Mokhtar said gruffly.

I smiled. "Someday I want to go to Paradise, but not tonight. I will visit New York City."

I was surprised at my words, though now that I had spoken them I realized that they had been in the back of my mind for a long time.

"I must go to New York," I told Shapoor when we were alone together. We sat on the front steps of our house and looked out toward the western hills, a smudge against the dark, star-pricked sky.

His voice was quiet. "Najmeh, we have no money."

"I know. I will fly now and pay later."

"The expenses while you are there?"

"Perhaps I have a little with my agent in New York. I will use that. Shapoor, I must try my best."

He took my hand and curled my fingers around his thumb. "I was just beginning to feel that you were mine again," he said. Then he dropped my hand and went into the dark house.

When I told my family of my plan to go again to America to talk to CARE about the factory, Fahkri said, "Najmeh-jun, you are without a mind. What will you gain from this trip? Nothing for yourself. It will take you months to get out of debt."

"Years," I agreed, "but I must go. I have tried to turn every stone here in Teheran and no stone will yield to me."

Then Fahkri's husband, always practical, asked, "Have you written for an appointment?"

"I'll not write because they could reply, 'Do not come.' If I telephone when I reach New York and they realize how much I have sacrificed to make the trip they will see me."

"You are wise but still you are foolish." Fahkri laughed.

Fahti moved uneasily. "Najmeh, should you leave Mother with the responsibility of the children?"

We were all concerned about the condition of Mother's leg. It was giving her more and more trouble. "Perhaps—" I began, but Mother said, "I will stay with the children. It is nothing. Ramazan and Nannie are there to help during the day and Shapoor leaves me little to do in the evening."

"I don't want to burden you," I said, leaning over to kiss her soft cheek.

"The children are never a burden," she told me. "You must do what you must do."

I made hasty arrangements to go to New York. Shortly I was back in Sarbandan. I had written CARE too late for them to advise against my coming, had called for an appointment after reaching New York City and had been courteously received by the director. First he had taken me for a tour of the plant. I had told him, "This is interesting but I have come a long way to discuss an important problem with you."

In his office we sat down together and he asked me a thousand questions—questions about cost breakdowns, marketing channels, all technical questions for which I had answers. We talked for three hours and in the end he promised that CARE would lend money for materials and further instruction and salaries, so that the looms could again sing and people work their way out of poverty.

In my room at the Y.W.C.A. I figured that each hour of this conference had cost me more than five hundred dollars.

The money had been promised in America but of course it would have to come through the CARE office in Teheran. Mr. Sakalis, who had shared my dream and made the building possible, was no longer in Iran. Assistant Director Davis, who had been my friend, had also left. Now I would have to work through a new administration.

This had been my life in Iran ever since I had returned from my school years in America! An old dream and a new administrator no matter from which department I sought help. It was late spring before I was able to see the new administrator, Dr. Kline.

When I was shown into his office my first impression was, What a handsome man Dr. Kline is! Perhaps he was forty-five, not older. He did not arise from his chair when I was introduced and I thought, This will be a short interview; he does not mean to give me much of his morning. My eyes went from his exactly right striped tie to the old ring on the well-shaped hand that sifted through the papers from the file on the Sarbandan project. He seemed aloof, somehow. Perhaps wary. He does not want to put his reputation—for he had made a great success of CARE projects in seven out of the fifteen areas in India—on a project that someone else has begun.

"CARE has already invested $16,000 in this project," he told me.

I nodded. "We have now a $16,000 shell with no life in it." I was not happy to be a person with my hand always out for a gift, my lips always begging for assistance; as I sat in Dr. Kline's office I saw in my imagination the endless stream of people who, like me, had passed before his desk, each asking for something, something that seemed to them to be of the greatest importance.

But Sarbandan is different, I reminded myself. And then I asked, "Have you time to hear the story of Sarbandan?"

"Certainly," he said, but the tone of his voice told me that he preferred short stories. So I spoke only of the factory, and of my hope for winter work for the women.

"How do the people of this village view the factory?" was his first question.

I told him of their giving land, of the women who eagerly learned how to weave, of their disappointment that the factory was not functioning, and of the village council's meeting that had pushed me into the decision to go to New York.

"I will give these reports my consideration," he said. And although he didn't stand I knew that the interview was closed.

"We will not speak again?" I asked.

"Call for an appointment." He sifted through the papers again and my eye was caught by the beautiful old ring. A man of taste, I thought. In any other situation except that of benefactor and benefited we could be friends.

When I kept my next appointment Dr. Kline rose to open the door for me, moved a comfortable chair near his desk and seated me before he drew up his own chair. His smile was a white flash in his suntanned face. He tapped the Sarbandan file with a perfectly manicured nail. "I like much of what I see here."

My whole concept of village work and Dr. Kline's seemed to be in harmony. Work, not bread, was what the people of Sarbandan needed and wanted—a chance to work and earn for themselves not only money and the necessities that money would buy, but self-confidence, pride, independence. There was much to discuss and it took many appointments to consider everything. Sometimes we met in the CARE office with my reports and CARE's papers before us. At times we took lunch or tea together. It was not long before I met his charming wife, Paula, and I knew immediately why this man and this woman had chosen each other.

It was spring before Dr. Kline went with Shapoor and me to Sarbandan. Together we walked along the narrow main street of the town where the jube is the center of all life. We sat in the teahouse of Mash'hadi Mokhtar. Both the tall Kadkhoda and the short Kadkhoda came to welcome him and through me he talked with them of the awakening that had come to the village in a little more than ten years. The women he saw only from a distance except for Zara, the brightest girl in the village, daughter of the big Kadkhoda and typical of the girls who would work in the factory. She answered some questions about the girls of the village while Asghar filled our tea glasses and passed tiny sweet cakes.

Above the village on a hill the silent factory stood, its windows like empty eyes looking across the village. After Dr. Kline had carefully inspected it we sat on the steps and looked over Sarbandan. Sarbandan is just one of hundreds of Persian villages, but one that had stirred to life and was ready to move into the modern world.

Back at my home we ate lamb korish together. "I am impressed by your aims," Dr. Kline told me. "But even more by your tenacity. I will do what I can. I'll try to get you the needed funds on a revolving loan, but, even more important, arrangements must be made to administer those funds directly."

Through the summer we saw Dr. Kline and his wife frequently and my admiration for both of them grew. Dr. Kline was not a man to move quickly, but once he decided what was right he would not agree to anything less.

It was not until autumn that he visited New York City and made the final arrangements for the $7,000 necessary to put the factory into operation.

Now the dream was so close that I could almost touch it.

15 ❧ The Sorrow

THERE CAME A NO RUZ WHEN THERE WAS NO HAPPINESS IN THE homes of my family; the throwing away of the sabzeh couldn't rid our homes of concern and sorrow. This new year it was not Mother who prepared the sabzeh for my children and for Mohsen's. Mohsen's wife and I had each put barley seed and water on an ancient Chinese plate from Mother's first set of dishes. The children had watched the red and gold Chinese men and women on the plate until the sprouting barley concealed the picture; then they had checked the growth of the sprouts that grew salad-green and healthy and had begged for a pink ribbon to tie around the mass, a ribbon "like Grandmother always used." But while they watched the sabzeh absorb the bickering and quarreling of the household they, themselves, had absorbed some of the anxiety of their parents.

Mother was ill, under the care of a doctor.

Mohsen called me one morning before I left for my office. "Najmeh-jun, are you all right?"

"Of course." But there was something in his voice that stirred me to greater uneasiness. "What is it, Mohsen?"

"It's Mother. The doctor was here last night and has been with her again this morning."

For some time, years perhaps, we had seen that Mother had trouble with her leg. She had walked about with increasing difficulty— and Mother loved to shop, to visit friends, to go to the public baths, to go to the mosque. I thought that Moshen spoke of the old trouble.

"Her leg?" I asked.

"This morning the doctor says there must be surgery immediately or she may lose her leg."

"No. There must be something else. Mother is aging. An operation might be too much for her."

Mohsen held himself to a patient explanation, speaking as if I were an idiot child. "Mother has had diabetes for a long time; the sugar which her body could not use has been stored in her blood. Since the circulation of blood in her leg has been so poor . . . Najmeh, you must make up your mind to this. . . . The doctors must do everything possible to encourage a stronger flow of blood or the leg will die, turn gangrenous, and she would lose it."

"But—" I persisted.

"Najmeh-jun, listen. We did not call the doctor because of Mother's leg. Already one thumb is gangrenous and must be removed. The surgery to help her leg can be done at the same time."

I listened in silence and even while I followed Mohsen's words a thousand pictures of Mother—pictures without continuity, without organization—flowed through my mind. How fast the mind travels from babyhood to just yesterday, from last year to the days of childhood. The memories separated me from the reality of Mohsen's words.

"Will you come now? Mother would like to be prepared for prayer before she leaves for the hospital. She is asking for you."

I turned to speak to Shapoor but he had either heard some of Mohsen's words or sensed the meaning of this conversation. "I am ready, Najmeh."

In the Volkswagen we took a short cut to Mohsen's house, bumping over unfinished streets of newer subdivisions, then, striking a main thoroughfare, slowing to an exasperating crawl as we cut through a herd of henna-decorated sheep on the way to market. We neither of us spoke, though anxiety was electric between us.

"Good morning, Mother," I said as I bent to kiss her soft cheek. In her eyes I saw peace, tranquillity, resignation. I helped her through her ablutions and prayers. My heart was praying, too, but in an unquiet, half-panicky way. It asked these questions; questions as old as the thinking of man: Why did this come to one so good, so faithful, so gentle as Mother? Is God, after all, just? Or perhaps He is helpless in this situation? And if He can't control something as minute as the sugar in one person's blood how, then, can He manage a universe? All of the time these thoughts were pressing against my faith I was repeating the words of faith and affirmation in prayer.

After we had given her into the care of the doctors we waited for the surgery to be completed and finally we saw her again. The operation had been successful; there was still to be much suffering.

As soon as the hospital would allow it I went to sit beside her. At times, between coma and consciousness, she would open her eyes and say, "O God, give me patience so I won't lose my faith." After a time when she was conscious for longer periods she would talk with us of our hopes and plans. In this emergency, when her thoughts should have turned inward, she was concerned with her inability to help us carry our loads.

Then in the middle of June Mother was again at Mohsen's home. True, she had to be lifted from her bed to the floor, from the floor to her bed. She could do none of the innumerable little services she had always done for us, but again she was the center of the life around her. None of us could believe that this was a terminal illness, that Mother had come home to die. She asked Mohsen to bring candies so that when the children came to see her there would be small treats. With her children and with Mohsen's daughter, Shahla, she talked in the same gentle, quiet way she had always talked, without bitterness, without sorrow. Often as I watched her placid face I thought of my own doubts the morning of her surgery. How could she be so sure of Allah and His watchful care?

One day when I went to visit her I saw her sitting up in bed with her small transistor radio in her hand; she was listening to the news. "Mother," I asked, "why do you want to know everything?"

She smiled, "This is my world, Najmeh. I must know what is happening to it."

So after the news was over I sat by her bed and told her of the work that went in and out of my office. I was working as an inspec-

tor for PLAN. The organization PLAN recommends the expenditure of large sums of money and one hundred fifty engineers and
doctors and one woman social worker—me—check on what the expenditure is accomplishing in providing clinics, baths, water systems, educational facilities.

"Twice a year I should travel around the country to see these
things with my own eyes."

Mother looked down at the bed, thinking, I know, of her inability to get up and take care of my home for me.

Her eyes filled with concern. Always she had said, "You go,
Najmeh. I will take care of things for you here."

I reassured her. "There is special pay for this travel so others
are glad to do it for me." We neither of us spoke of the change her
illness had brought into all of our lives. We talked, instead, of the
need for inspectors. "Everywhere it is the same," I told Mother.
"Not in Iran alone. A few years ago when I was a secretary in the
office of the Prime Minister many unemployed men came from
Yazd. They weren't asking for a gift. They wanted work so that
they could feed their families."

"The people of Yazd are the most honest hardworking people in
Iran," Mother commented.

"They were set to digging for water near Abassabad. When they
found that there was no water where they were digging they sent a
delegation to the government. Some wit told them, 'Be quiet. The
project might not bring water but it brings bread.' In another area less
honest contractors were hired to dig for water. When PLAN inspectors checked on the use of money that had been allotted for water
pumps, for electrification and digging and found that the work was
a failure the contractors replied, 'We were hired for digging, not
necessarily for bringing up water.' "

"Najmeh-jun," Mother asked, "can inspectors, laws, government
policy make honest men?"

"No." I was silent for a time. "All these may help but it is
education, the lessening of poverty—" Abruptly I stopped talking
of these distant things and started speaking of the factory. "Honesty
increases as need decreases," I said, and I hoped that I was right, for

my whole philosophy of work for my people depended upon this premise. "Some men have a memorial built to them, Mother," I said, "but I will finish this factory and it will be a memorial to you."

She smiled but shook her head. "My grave will be in the loving hearts of my children."

As concerned as I was about the factory and about Sarbandan I made few trips to the village. I didn't want to be far away from the telephone. Once as I was leaving the office one of the other workers who had asked me to stop for tea said, "Don't you dread these visits to your mother?"

"They are my greatest delight," I told her, and I realized with a rush of love and sorrow that I spoke the truth.

And yet there were things that had to be done in Sarbandan. It seemed as if we would never get the Sarbandan co-op correctly registered. Time and again I had brought some of the villagers to Teheran at my own expense to appear before committees, to answer questions, to present the attitude of the villagers toward the cooperative. One afternoon Shapoor drove me to Sarbandan to stay over Friday with the hope that somehow we could go forward with this worrisome business.

Since I had left Ramazan and Nannie with the children I sent for Asghar to prepare a tea for us and do the other things that were needed.

"I am so tired," I told Shapoor and Asghar, "I will see no one this evening and tomorrow we shall begin early since there is so much to be done."

Shapoor's face mirrored his worry as he looked at me and I tried to smile back to dispel the worry before I went to my room and lay upon my bed trying to relax and close out all troublesome thoughts from my mind and heart.

There was a timid knock on the door. Asghar or Shapoor? It was Asghar who put his head around the door frame. "Lady Najafi, please see Davud. His trouble is deep."

Davud—not one of the council so his problem must be a personal one. Evidently it was a pressing one, too, or he would not present himself so late in the evening. I put on my shoes and retied the white chiffon scarf over my head before I left my room. Davud was sitting on the floor, his feet crossed under him in the Persian manner, but his head was bent forward until it was almost against the floor and his face was in his hands. He didn't look up when I entered but when I spoke he lifted a face so distorted with grief that it was hardly recognizable. I wondered at once what member of his family had died, and yet his face mirrored helpless anger as well as grief.

"Lady Najafi, what shall I do? It is my daughter, my little Turan."

"What has happened to Turan?"

"She has made a bad marriage. Her husband is killing her."

I remembered Turan at the time of her wedding, less than a month ago it seemed, fourteen or perhaps only thirteen but so proudly riding upon the decorated horse that was taking her to the home of her husband.

"Does he beat her?" I asked gently, and I remembered a beautiful young wife in Dashte Moghan who came to our classes bruised and bleeding from the hands of her husband. We had gone to her father with an account of the husband's cruelty. He not only beat her every day but clutched her by her long hair and dragged her through her house and into her courtyard. The father said, "She left my home in her wedding veil and she will return only in her shroud."

But Davud was different.

"Tell me," I said gently, "just what has happened to little Turan."

"She has been beaten again and again by her husband. It is not just. She has always been such a sweet, good child. He took her to Teheran and we thought things might be better for her in the home of his sister but his sister's husband has also beaten her. When she became ill he sent her home."

"What is the reason for this?"

"He says she does not give the satisfaction a husband must have from a wife."

"Is Turan in your home now? I will go with you."

Shapoor brought my jacket and the three of us walked out into the quiet night. There is so much peace in a mountain village asleep under the deep star-pierced Persian sky that it seems incredible that there may also be cruelty, brutality.

Davud pushed aside the gelim that covered the doorway of his house and I went into the little lantern-lighted room. I knelt by Turan, lying on a pallet on the dirt floor. "Turan," I said softly, "tell me what has happened?"

She moaned and tossed her head, biting her lip as if to keep from crying out. I put my hand on her forehead and it felt like a burning coal.

"Shapoor," I said, turning to him, "will you tell the doctor that we are bringing Turan to the clinic?"

"What can a doctor do with a man who beats his wife into her grave?" Davud asked angrily.

"Come, this is no time for anger. You and I wll carry Turan to the clinic."

"I, myself, will carry her," Davud said. "She is scarcely heavier than when she was a little child." The tears rolled down his cheeks as he took her pitifully thin body into his arms.

We laid Turan on the examination table and the doctor said, "Lady Najafi and I must be alone wth Turan. We must see what causes this fever and delirium."

Quickly he made a routine check—temperature, pulse, blood pressure, then gently, ever so gently, he examined her bruised and welted body and after a time said, "These people do not understand that to a doctor the body of a woman is a problem, not an excitement. Turan has a serious infection. She has been brutally deflowered."

"I cannot understand," I told him.

"I, myself, have never seen it; but there are men who are incapable for some physical reason of the marriage relationship. This husband

could be such a person. He would blame his own failure to find satisfaction on his wife and his frustration would speak in brutal acts."

I rearranged her clothing.

"She cannot be cared for here; she needs a hospital. I will give her an injection to fight the blood poisoning and one to relieve the pain but you must take her to Damavand."

While I spoke to Shapoor the doctor spoke to the parents.

"In a hospital," he told her parents—and they both began to object but he finished his sentence—"they may perhaps save little Turan's life."

A Volkswagen doesn't make a good ambulance but we did the best we could to make the child comfortable. In the hospital at Damavand we learned that the doctor's diagnosis had been correct. Turan had been brutally deflowered with some unclean knife. There was infection of the wound and general blood poisoning. The young doctor who made the report to us said, "This I have never seen before. It does not occur in our villages in the North where I came from."

"It does not happen—" I began to say; then I realized that as long as I had known my village, as closely as I had worked with my people, I could not know what was in every heart.

When I returned to Teheran without accomplishing anything for the Sarbandan cooperative I was deeply shaken, so went, of course, to the room of my mother. She was asleep, a calm smile on her pale face. When she stirred and reached for my hand I asked, "Mother, what do you dream of as you smile in your sleep?"

"I dream that in the morning Mohsen will open the door, bring my tray of food and sit me on the floor for my early prayers. While I am out of my bed he will make it and I will watch him and be proud that he is my son. Sometimes I dream that you or Shahla or one of the others opens my door and I am proud and happy because you are gifts from God."

I tried to speak lightly to forget the horror of the night. "You are a proud woman, Mother."

"Am I, Najmeh? But perhaps one must be proud. Proud of patience, courage, ability to forgive others and never hold evil in the heart."

I took the brush from Mother's dressing table and began to brush her long, silver hair. As I braided it in a wide braid to lay over her shoulder I asked, "Of beauty, Mother?"

She smiled, "Maybe once upon a time."

At my desk I held my mind to the reports that needed my consideration and yet I telephoned each day to the Damavand hospital. Turan would live; the blood poisoning was controlled by the new drugs. Her mind? Perhaps. The experience, so traumatic, would not be easily forgotten. Yet she was young. I telephoned Mohsen's home. I kept in touch with my own home and tried to carry on the work of Sarbandan. "Najmeh-jun," Shapoor said when he took me in his arms to find me quivering with fatigue, "you are riding for a fall."

When Mother had been out of the hospital for six weeks, moved by some premonition, she decided to spend some time in the home of each of her children. Her heart turned with special fondness to Shahla, Mohsen's golden-haired, green-eyed daughter. Mother had reared her after the death of Mohsen's first wife and she was like another daughter. I often thought, too, that Mother might have seen herself as a young bride since she, too, had been a blonde with delicate beauty. Though Shahla was just nineteen she already had a son of three and a daughter one and a half, and she was expecting another infant.

After two weeks with Shahla she asked to come to me. We had done everything we could to prepare a pleasant place for her, putting her bed in our salon, where everything the eye touched would be beautiful. But she came bringing candies and toys for the children, doing all she could to make the visit pleasant for us. Nassim and Sina ran laughing and shouting to her. How they had missed her. She didn't seem like an invalid, a person near death. The day after her arrival she sat on a bench in the garden watching the children laughing and playing in the pool. Later we ate dinner with invited guests and her presence in our home was like a benediction. After dinner, when Mohsen, his wife and the other guests had left, Mother said, "Shapoor, will you turn my bed?"

"Surely," he said, and he was on his feet in an instant. "How do you want it turned?"

"Please turn it toward Mecca."

I helped her to prepare for bed, but she wanted first to sit upon the floor for prayer. I sat close beside her as she read from the Koran and went through her prayers. Tonight her prayers were unusual. Quietly, without passion, she asked Allah to forgive her faults and her sins. Finally she said, "Najmeh, I am ready," and we helped her to bed, where she lay facing Mecca. I knelt close beside her and read a special prayer. Many years before, when I was in America, Mother had sent me a tiny Koran on a chain. This I had worn on my breast when my babies were born. I fastened it on Mother's neck and her fingers, still straight and supple, caressed the jewel-like cover. Almost at once she fell asleep.

I tiptoed away so as not to disturb her. The children were in bed, still laughing and playing as unsupervised children will, so I went to them and said, "Grandmother is sleeping now. If you love her be silent."

The next morning Fahkri came to take Mother to her home. "She still sleeps," I said.

"It is time she wakened," Fahkri said. She went to the door and said gently, "Mother, Mother." When there was no answer she went in. "Najmeh, she is dead. Mother is dead!" She screamed and began to moan in a way that would shatter the heart of God.

I put my arms around her. "Fahkri, we must keep ourselves strong. We must not show these passions before the dead."

I went into the room and looked upon my mother's face. Never had it been more peaceful. It was as if she slept with the most pleasant dreams, or perhaps too deep for dreaming. I kissed her cold face. With the help of Nannie and Ramazan we put her bed in the center of the room and then the servants carried out the vases, the decorative boxes, every delicate thing that decorated the salon.

"I must call Shapoor," I told Fahkri, sobbing in a corner of the room. But first I called Mohsen. The moment he heard my voice on the telephone he said, "Little Sister, is it Mother?"

"In her sleep."

"I'll come at once."

"Mohsen, bring her shroud."

It is the custom in my country to buy the shroud long before one is in need of it, selecting it with care. If possible it is taken to a holy place, Ghom, Najaf, Mashed, and blessed for this special use. Often it is of cotton like a white bed sheet. Mother had selected a soft cashmere in creamy white.

"Be comforted," Mohsen said quietly. "We have expected this."

But when Mohsen came into my home and saw the bed in the middle of the room as it must be for the dead, he struck his head against the wall so hard I feared the head would break. There is a moment of realization far different from the anticipation of the event. I wondered if that moment had yet come to me as I went about without weeping, without tears.

Soon Shapoor was beside me; the home was filled with the family. Shahla was there, her long golden hair streaming across Mother's pillow as she buried her face in her grandmother's neck. "I loved her so," Shahla repeated over and over again while her tears wet the pillow.

"If Mother had known that the children would be so unhappy she wouldn't have died," I said, and then I wondered why I had said such a foolish thing. It was only that Mother never did give sorrow to others.

Nassim and Sina were frightened. I took them to the bench in the garden and tried to tell them about the Moslem idea of death. I told them that a part of their grandmother that we could not see would walk in a beautiful garden under deep shade of flowering trees. That gentle waters would flow through the garden and the music of birds would be everywhere. There would be soft grass to cushion the feet and their grandmother would be able to walk again. They listened with their trustful eyes on my face, and I thought, Either this is a beautiful story or it is the only true reality.

I searched my heart and found that I believed that Mother was in this place where pain and grief are left behind.

I left the children sitting together on the bench talking to each other of this beautiful land that Sina thought must be like the California of which we had so often spoken.

At noon the Mullah came for the special prayer in the house of the dead. I prepared Mother for her last journey. There must be no rings on the ears, no chains at the throat, no jewels on the fingers when the body is returned to the dust.

The sons and the sons-in-law carried the bier. Near the cemetery we stopped at the house for the washing of the dead. This I wanted to do myself for my mother. Carefully I washed the body that for so long had been the home of a beautiful spirit, which at one time had been my own home, and I wondered why even now I could not cry. I wrapped her in the shroud, tying it over her feet and over her head. It was Mohsen and my older brother, Ali, who lowered the body into the grave. Sina tugged at my black chadar. "Is this Grandmother?" he wanted to know. "Is it?" Evidently he had been expecting to see the beautiful garden I had described.

Everybody threw a little earth into the grave. "Yes, Sina, this is Grandmother's body. This is the place that Grandmother is going to stay."

"No," Sina protested. "Not here." And all of our hearts echoed the little child's protest.

We returned to my home, allowing ourselves to grieve. There were two hundred people in the house and garden. All were trying to eat luncheon from a great cloth spread on the floor. On it was every variety of excellent food: fruit, bread, cheese, cakes. My sisters-in-law had arranged for this with the help of the cook or houseboy from every home. For three days there was food upon the cloth for anyone who came to grieve with us. Then the cloth was folded as a sign that the mourning was finished, but in my heart I knew that I had not even begun to mourn.

For three days the talk had been of my mother, who knew most of the people in the town: how there was a smile on her face for everybody, rich or poor; how she loved everybody as if all men were her children; how she helped the poor with money, the sorrowing with comfort, the discouraged with helpful words. The women spoke of the chadars she had cut and made for her daughters and for many others that we might be suitably covered for prayer.

On the 15th of August the announcement of Mother's death was made in the Teheran papers. "Mr. Mohsen Najafi announces the death—" and then followed an announcement from each of us. Seeing the announcement in the paper all who knew even one of us would come to give sympathy at one of the two memorial services. For the men a great service would be held in the mosque at the bazaar. There the men of the family would stand near the entrance and accept the sympathy of friends. Inside the mosque there would be readings from the Koran, drinking of tea. The memorial service for the women would be held in my home and there was much preparation necessary. Still it seemed as if someone had struck me a heavy blow and I was only partly conscious. I could not weep as the others did, lessening their grief through its expression; I rationalized that I must be controlled and gracious, keeping everything in quietness. I felt that I had swallowed some deadly potion that left me only half alive, half alert. Yet, when Shapoor's mother came into the room with one of her daughters and, passing around the circle of mourners, offered me her hand and spoke gently to me, this movement toward healing the break between us found an awakened place my heart and I was grateful.

After seven days there was a visit to the grave. There were beautiful Persian rugs on the grave and bowls of fruit. There were tea and coffee for everyone. The service was long—perhaps two hours—but still I watched quietly. Abruptly I felt that tears were coming down my cheeks; the dreadful dam in my heart had given away and now the good, strong pain of my bereavement shook me.

When forty days had passed there would be another service. After a year another. It is not until the heart is broken that it can mend again. Forty days were given to quietness, to grief, to contemplation. During these forty days I had the apartness from life that I needed to look at myself through different eyes. Always I had thought of myself as Najmeh, an independent person, myself. Now I saw myself as an extension, in many ways, of my mother. When as a young girl I had wanted to open a modiste shop she had said, "It is good. Najmeh is young but she knows what is best for her." And I hadn't wondered if sometime behind that close-held chadar Mother had longed to be out in the world, a part of it. When I had wanted to go to America to study she had held the Koran for me to kiss and had splashed on me the drops of water that said, "May God be with you. May God travel with you." But I hadn't thought that through me Mother, too, was traveling to this different land. When I had returned home she had kissed me and said, "I thought that the day might never come when my eyes would see you again, Najmeh-jun." She had blessed my departure with these misgivings in her heart. When I had wanted to work in Sarbandan she had supported me in my plan and later when I was called to Baluchistan she had taken the children to make my work possible. Finally, when I had left my home, Shapoor, the children, she had stepped in to hold things together for me until my return.

For the forty days of quietness I lived with my mother in memory; still many hours were empty and desolate. When I felt her close to me I was warmed and encouraged by her confidence in my dedication, my perseverance, perhaps my abilities, and I resolved to carry my plans to fulfillment for her sake. The factory must be finished as she had dreamed that it would be. I must make Sarbandan a symbol of what awakened villages in Iran can be when they emerge from medieval times into the modern world. These projects were Mother's projects, too.

There was another facet of Mother's life that I must live with more closely—the warm, wise human being. I must educate myself to accept those things in my life that cannot be changed. I must give more love to more people—especially to those nearest me.

After forty days I came back into the world as a spring breaks through its winter fetters of ice.

But one day when I came home from the office Nassim brought me a letter she had written. "I wrote this for Grandmother. You must mail it for me."

16 ❧ The Fright

WITH THE MONEY BORROWED FROM CARE TO COMPLETE THE equipping of the factory and to buy raw materials, Sarbandan came alive. First the building must be repaired because the walls had suffered some winter damage and the broken roof must be mended. How willing the men were to make these repairs now that hope was lighting the village. Our first weaving teacher had left and we had to search for another. Finally, also from the North, came Solomon. He, too, had the small eyes and the large nose of the North; he, too, was not beautiful, but he was expert and patient. When he began to thread the looms he found that some parts were missing. It took three months to order these parts and receive them in Sarbandan. Three months while everyone waited, some doubters openly prophesying that we would never use the factory.

While we waited for the parts I contacted many of the textile factories of my country. I had spent some time visiting such factories in India and in Japan but now I must know what materials, what designs would market well in Iran. The factory must not fail because the business was not well handled and several individuals whom I had contacted offered special services without charge. My sister Fahkri's husband, Engineer Asbaghi, prepared the texts of the contracts; bookkeeping was organized by Engineer Abuzari; marketing and color design were handled by Engineer Seyavashi.

Everyone responded to the feeling of progress that had shaken the village. Nearly every week Musi left me a message requesting my immediate presence in Sarbandan.

"Does Mash'hadi Mokhtar have you on a string that you should dance like a puppet to his every request?" Shapoor asked.

"I am happy to dance as long as the music is cheerful," I said.

The next Friday as we drove up before the teahouse the news was that the Department of Education had sent additional teachers to the school for boys. I didn't dampen Mash'hadi Mokhtar's joy in telling me this by saying that I had already known of the government's literacy corp, which our Shah hopes will reduce the illiteracy in all the villages of Iran.

The factory, the clinic, the school, but still all was not Paradise. As the work on the factory was finished came the argument and strife that I hadn't even considered. Who would be the manager of the factory? Mash'hadi Mokhtar, of course, he told everybody who stopped in at the teahouse. Had he not proven himself to be a competent manager with his teahouse, his bus line, his farm, his large family of brothers and sisters as well as his own children, for whom he made wise decisions? Had he not always been the first to offer land for village improvements? He never neglected to take his gold crowns from their tray each morning and slip them over his front teeth in order to be his most impressive best, and the gold teeth flashed under his magnificent mustache as he passed the tea glasses.

Mohradi, of course. Was he not the tall Kadkhoda and the most important man of the village, to whom everyone looked with respect? Mash'hadi Mokhtar did well with his own business, but the factory was a village affair and the management should certainly be in the hands of the community leader. Mohradi was slightly inconvenienced since he had no tea to pass out, no comfortable room in which the old men could gather for business and gossip. But perhaps he had other favors . . .

Kutchiki, the short Kadkhoda, did not push his claim. Everyone knew that he was a competent man, especially with the shepherds and the herds in the summer. If there were any who did not know they could listen to his mother, his other relatives.

And how about Ali? Had he not been the caretaker of the factory all the years that it stood vacant and had he not done a careful, painstaking job? Had any vandal broken a window of the factory, defaced its clean walls, or broken in to damage the looms?

No one in the village had even thought of bringing a stranger to the factory to be its manager. This I had thought of and discussed with Shapoor and with others interested in the project. Bringing in an expert manager would certainly have advantages. Yet, since I had often been the stranger with technical expertness, I knew from my own experience how slowly an ingrown village accepts anyone from outside.

The meeting of the stockholders, really a meeting of the Rish e safed under a different name for this particular meeting, was the most exciting one I had ever attended.

After the usual formalities the new business was quietly introduced. At once there were half a dozen men wanting to take the floor to speak for themselves or for a favorite candidate. All of the arguments for Mash'hadi Mokhtar, for Mohradi, for Kutchiki and for Ali were advanced with passion. Each of the men, with the exception of Kutchiki, looked to me for support.

Once, years ago, I had felt that an organized cooperative would succeed in Sarbandan only if it was headed by someone in whom all the villagers had trust, not some organizer from outside the village. When a course for supervisors of cooperatives was organized I had walked up to the mountain cabin of Kutchiki. Leaning against the rock wall of the sheep enclosure I had talked with him about the cooperative. I had told him that the Rish e safed felt that he was the one person in Sarbandan who could take this training and head the cooperative. Although he had said warily, "What can a man do in Sarbandan after he has been Kadkhoda?" he had left his position and gone to Teheran.

Very soon he had returned to Sarbandan, his face tight and angry. We learned that the foundation had turned him down in Teheran. There was a rule that every entrant must have six years of schooling. At that time only four years were offered in Sarbandan but I had thought his experience as Kadkhoda would be considered an equivalent of two years in elementary school. But the foundation had held to the rules and the slight young man who had gone off with the happiest face had come home with a face filled with pain.

Later when I had spoken to him and practically insisted on an answer he had told me, "It is said that two beggars can sleep on the same rug, but two kings cannot live in the same country." He had thought that two Kadkhodas in Sarbandan had made things more difficult for me and that I had plotted to remove him by getting him to resign on what I knew to be a false promise. Later he had taken sheep to the mountains, his own and the flocks of others, and still later he had been reinstated as Kadkhoda of the mountain villagers in Sarbandan.

Now during the discussion of who should be manager of the factory he carefully kept his eyes from mine. I had been blameless in the other matter, but he would never believe that and now he would not give me his trust.

"What do you think, Lady Najafi? You have had experience in these things," Jamshid, the oldest man among the stockholders, asked.

"This is for you to decide. This is your factory. Let each man be nominated by one who knows his qualities. Then, remembering that we have borrowed money from CARE, that this money was not given to us, decide. The position of manager is not a gift that should be given to any man without careful thought."

Then came an argument louder and more vociferous than business arguments should be. It was true that Mash'hadi Mokhtar was the wealthiest man in the village as he was always willing to declare. It was true he had been the first to give land, labor, encouragement in the form of hard-to-come-by money. It was also true that he was so busy with his own affairs that the factory would come second. It was true that Mohradi, tall Kadkhoda, managed the village with fairness and with strength; but didn't this take all of his time? What would happen to the village while he worked at the factory?

It was true that . . .

So I said, "There are many who know the business of factories, of weaving, of looms. One of these we could employ to come to the factory. In Isfahan there are many such men. In Azerbaijan—"

Of course, they were all agreed that the manager must come from the village. And so how about Kutchiki? He was a man of great integrity, an intelligent man, a man who could take time from his duties to operate the factory. Perhaps Mohradi could increase his own work enough to manage the mountain part of the village when Kutchiki was busy with the factory.

Besides, Kutchiki spoke Turkish, and our instructor would, if he came from the North, speak Turkish. Solomon already needed a translator if he spoke anything but the simplest words.

There was an almost unanimous vote for Kutchiki, and Mash'-hadi Mokhtar, his face purple with anger, rose from his place on the floor. He had walked to the door before he turned and said, "None of my family will ever work in this factory."

After he left, the meeting was silent for a moment as if we had entered the eye of a windstorm. I knew that Mash'hadi Mokhtar would not live by this threat. He loved money and he would not be likely to close the hands of his family when money was in sight. Then, too, he was wise enough to know that the feeling of freedom was growing in the village as it progressed. His hold on his brothers was growing more precarious every day, and soon he might feel the same rebellion in his sons and daughters if his choices for them were not wise ones.

Of course I knew that the factory might have an expert, too. One who knew materials and markets, methods and men. But this could be taken care of quietly—later.

Then the men fell to arguing about who would operate the looms. Should the workers be men or women? Should the families of stockholders be chosen to sit at the looms before others were given that opportunity?

Wearily I said, "For tonight we have had enough discussion. Now we will have tea, and perhaps sweets."

The men still sat in a circle on the floor of my meeting room but with their hands nursing the hot tea glasses their voices were quieter. They turned to discussing two by two the defeat of Mash'hadi Mokhtar, who never before had been defeated.

But adjourning the meeting didn't solve the problem of which women, which girls, which boys should be employed at the looms. The next morning before I had left the house to walk around the village Mr. Nadaff, the dehyar, was at the door. "Lady Najafi," he said, "May I talk with you?"

"I was about to walk up to the factory," I told him, "but come in and sit down. Have you had tea?"

"I'll walk along with you," he suggested, "since I wanted to talk about the factory. Kutchiki is a good choice, I think. How did you get the men to select him?"

I thought of Shapoor's accusing me of "controlling" the men, and said rather shortly, "I said nothing."

"It is well that the important positions in the village are distributed," he continued. "Mash'hadi Mokhtar, to his own enterprises, Mohradi to the government of the village, Kutchiki to the factory."

I knew this was not what Mr. Nadaff had come so early in the morning to tell me so I was silent.

"And the positions in the factory should be distributed in the same way. The work should be planned so that one person from each family in the village may earn a salary."

I smiled. "There are five hundred families in the village."

"Well, then, not more than one person from any family."

"Mr. Nadaff, you have been in the village two years. You have been very wise in working with the men. They trust you and cooperate with you. I know the women."

"You will talk to the women, then. For my part I hear nothing but contention."

I thought of the $7,000 we had borrowed from CARE, of Dr. Kline's confidence in the project and in me. Contention could ruin everything we planned to do. "I'll speak to the women. Tell them to come to me with their arguments."

"Look," I told a group of women who had gathered around the front porch of my home asking who would earn money in the factory that all had helped to build, "it seems to you the fair way, the right way to run the factory is to choose one from each family that needs employment, in order to share the earnings equally. But this is not the only way. A girl works in the factory. Zorah, here, for example. She is very efficient. Her hands fly. She makes no mistakes. Nothing that she weaves must be undone. And she earns, let us say, forty rials a day. This she gives to her mother. Her mother has shoes repaired for the children, so money goes to the shoemaker; she buys sugar and tea, so money goes to the shopkeeper; she buys a bit of lamb for dinner, and the money goes to the owner of the lamb and to the keeper of the abattoir. Perhaps her husband must go to Teheran on the bus or he may wish to drink tea in the teahouse and some of the money goes to Mash'hadi Mokhtar. Can you understand these things?"

"We understand," some of the women said, but still they went away grumbling. It seemed to them as if the gate to Paradise had been open and I had closed it to them. The clinic, the school—these were for everybody. They had thought that the factory would be open in the same way, and they could not understand how competence should make any difference in employment. To these people who had had so little—many women had never handled any money at all—economic interdependence was completely out of their experience and understanding. I knew that I had not heard the last of this problem as a group of women gathered around Eshrat to hear what she had to say. Eshrat, I decided, should be employed in the factory, if only to keep all matters of contention close to my ears.

One afternoon I had had a long meeting with the stockholders. The factory had been running for some time. Already we were producing a natural muslin of great strength, an attractive black and white herringbone material suitable for many uses, and beautiful red, blue and white tweedlike material. We were also manufacturing gelims, a kind of blanket that should be attractive to foreign buyers. We were now planning a formal opening at which our factory as well as the goods we produced would be exhibited to CARE officials, the press and other guests from Teheran. I had taken my vacation to prepare for this opening and the meeting was the first step in preparation.

I had been making assignments for special tasks. We must have chairs, cabinets, a clock, pictures of the Shah, flags, samovars, dishes, refreshments. We must send invitations to the guests. Everybody must do something toward the great day. Some would do the shopping, others would perform other chores. By the time the meeting was over I was trembling with fatigue. "You must come and go to bed at once," Shapoor told me. "I will bring a tea to the bed."

And Mohsen who had come with us said, "Najmeh-jun, you will kill yourself, then who will profit?"

The next morning, Friday, Shapoor and Mohsen left early for Teheran and I, wanting to be alone, walked up to the factory, which on Friday should be silent. But as I walked some of the women and girls joined me. "Is it right," Eshrat, always difficult, asked, "that Zorah should make twice as much as I do? She is only a girl and I am a woman."

"Zorah works much faster."

"I work as fast as I can and still do the work well," Eshrat insisted.

"Zorah does the work well and she does more in a day."

I tried to explain piecework to Eshrat, but from my first days in Sarbandan Eshrat had been reluctant to learn. Now I had hurt her pride and several of her friends began to talk loudly, seemingly to Eshrat but their words were meant for my ears. Quietly I walked on up the path. Abruptly I lost all patience. "This is the way it is. This way will not be changed." Too tired to listen to another word, I walked into the factory and closed the door behind me and locked it. The last shift of the day before had left the weaving room out of order. I began to pick up a few tools. This led to my sweeping the place. No one uses a long-handled Western broom in Iran; one must stoop low or squat on one's heels to sweep. As I bent to the task my nose began to bleed, just a few drops against my white handkerchief. I left the factory and hurried to my home on the other side of the village. Before I arrived there, the blood was dropping, dropping. I had thought of stopping at the clinic but all

I really wanted was to be at home lying on my own bed.

When I passed the Kadkhoda's house, Zorah, his daughter, saw my blood-drenched handkerchief and sent one of her little brothers racing for the doctor. He must have shouted as he ran because I had scarcely fallen upon my bed when a crowd began to gather outside my front door. The doctor came running. How grateful I was for this clean, competent man! "We must pack the nose and encourage the blood to clot. I wish I had the correct supplies."

"I have something," I told him.

Zorah had followed the doctor into the room and stood sniffling away tears. I directed her to bring a box of Tampax from my storage chest.

"This is right. This is good," he said. But the packing forced into the nostrils was soon soaked with blood and the blood running warm and salty down my throat was making me desperately ill. "We will try this," the doctor said, giving me a hypodermic injection, but this too failed.

I began to feel as if I might bleed to death here in the house that Shapoor and I had built to our love.

Mash'hadi Mokhtar and Musi had been outside the house with the rest of the villagers. Now they came and stood beside my bed, Mash'hadi looking at me with the kindliness of a father. "I must go to Teheran to a hospital," I told them. "Bring the bus."

"The bus will cost one hundred toman," Musi said, but Mash'-hadi Mokhtar signaled him to be quiet. Mash'hadi, Musi and the young teacher carried me in their arms to the bus and the villagers watched me carried as I had carried so many of their sick children. They made a lane of lighted lanterns for us to pass through and a murmur of commiseration sounded to me like the faraway sound of Moslem mourning.

We left at ten and by one I was in the hospital at Teheran. Even the doctors there could not stop the bleeding at once and I was unconscious when Mohsen came, bringing flowers, and Shapoor slipped in to sit beside me.

What had caused my illness? Overwork, the doctors said, tensions, anxiety. My blood pressure was extremely high. I was fortunate that the blood had rushed to the outside through my nose rather than sweeping across my brain. Now two months of complete rest were indicated.

Rest? How could I rest with the factory opening so soon? With work piling up on my office desk? With Shapoor, Sina and Nassim depending on me? As I lay quietly on the hospital bed I wanted to live, with all my heart I wanted to live. I wanted to see the factory registered as a weaving and training center and CARE repaid the money we had borrowed. I wanted to make a better life for Shapoor and to rear my family to maturity.

I wondered which of these hopes came first. I still could not honestly say.

17 ❧ An End and a Beginning

SHAPOOR AND I STOOD SIDE BY SIDE ON THE PORCH OF OUR SARBAN-dan home to welcome our guests to the formal opening of the factory. First there would be luncheon in the home, then all of the guests would walk through the town to the factory for the official inauguration. If I turned my head I could see through the open door my mother-in-law and my three girls, Farkandah, Effat and Pooran, busy in the reception room. For forty days I had been preparing for this reception and Fahti had cooked in her home day after day, but to have Shapoor's mother sharing in our project—this was something that warmed me through and gave me a special lilting happiness.

It was late Mehr, October, almost wintertime. Always before in Aban, November, the village had sunk into its winter sleep. But this year, 1965, would be different. Still, many of the men would go away to Mazandaran, but the factory would be the center of a new life. The song of the shuttle would be heard in the silence of the snow. Young people would leave Sarbandan—girls and boys—but now, instead of seeking low-paid common labor in the rice fields or as servants in Teheran, they would go into positions that could utilize their skills. Already five girls and four boys, carrying my special recommendation with them, had found weaving to do in Teheran factories at twice the pay we could afford in Sarbandan. Typical of these young people was Gholan Reza. Perhaps he had inherited from his father, the village shoemaker, special dexterity with his hands; he was so much faster than the others. He learned to produce two gelims in one day and in Teheran earned nine toman

202

each day. Three toman were needed for his board and room with a family; the rest he sent home to help support his five brothers and sisters. What a difference his help would make to the family. There would be rice and bread and occasionally meat; there would be shoes and clothing for the children so that they could all attend school.

Perhaps Sarbandan would become a training center instead of just a production center, thus outgrowing my dream. Once I had thought that the factory would keep young people at home; now I saw it as a door to the better things in the outside world.

As I stood beside my husband I thought of how dreams change and grow. Never is a dream fulfilled before it has been supplanted by one of larger dimensions. Not even dreams are static.

For forty days the villagers had been busy cleaning the mosque, the bath, the clinic, their own homes, their latrines, the streets, the bed of the jube. They had repaired broken walls and buried debris in the fields and gardens. To our visitors this would seem to be the cleanest village in Iran. The people had also cleansed themselves and their patched clothing, and the children were smiling and shining.

"It looks as if we were getting ready to be reviewed by the Shah," Mash'hadi Mokhtar grumbled.

"There is an old saying that the King's eyes and ears are everywhere in the land," I told him.

At about noon the visitors from Teheran began to arrive in transportation furnished by CARE. Dr. Kline was traveling outside of Iran and I wished deeply that he could have seen this thing that his interest had brought to life. But there were many more guests: people from CARE, from all of the agencies interested in rural development; there were factory owners who would be interested in our training program and others who had advised us or helped us as we built and equipped the factory. There were newsmen and photographers. To all we offered our hands. My heart was skipping even as my throat swelled with glad tears.

After they had greeted us they passed inside to the feast. And what a beautiful feast! Shapoor's mother and Fahti are both specially gifted in the preparation of excellent food, and the table, beautifully decorated, was covered with appetizing dishes.

My girls had come "home" to Sarbandan, too. Effat, who now has a husband who is also a social worker and three sons, had come from the Garmsar area. Farkandah, now a supervisor of schools and women's activities, the wife of a project superintendent and the mother of two children, had come from the Varamin area. And Pooran, little Pooran who is now supervisor of women's activities with nine girls working under her direction, appearing on radio every week to describe her activities, had come from Gavin bringing Homah with her. Homah had never worked in Sarbandan but in any village she fits like the jewel in a ring. In the Gavin area she had developed the best kindergarten in the villages of Iran.

I had had little time to talk with the girls, but we had figured that the original three that had begun their study in Sarbandan had now grown to more than a hundred trained either by me or by one of my girls.

Now they were assisting in serving our guests and filling the house with their gaiety and charm.

When everyone had eaten and one guest had found a ja-jim and crawled under it in a corner to sleep, the rest of the party walked through the village. The stockholders, their wives and children joined us as we moved uphill toward the factory. Eagerly they drank in the praise that was given to the village.

The people of Sarbandan waited outside while the guests inspected the factory, examining the looms and the other equipment, touching with admiring fingers the samples of work we had on display.

Then we all stood outside where all could see the plaques, one in Farsi, the other in English:

CARE A GIFT OF THE PEOPLE OF THE UNITED STATES

Standing on the steps, the tears coming from my heart into my voice, I gave a short speech:

"I wish to thank the ladies and gentlemen from Teheran and my people of Sarbandan who have come here today to help me to put my head in the heavens.

"For the information of our very distinguished and dear guests I must make a brief speech.

"After studies in the village of Sarbandan and neighboring villages I decided since the construction of a bathhouse, a clinic and other facilities was completed I should take steps to begin a project that would have a lasting effect on the life of the village people from an economic point of view. For this reason a plan for establishing a small factory was decided upon and was suggested to the village council and the village people who make up the cooperative. The village people were glad to put their feet ahead with this project and donated sixteen thousand meters of land for this purpose. The ministry of roads prepared the ground for future building. With the help of PLAN Organization and the cooperation of friends, particularly Engineer Mahadavi, the architectural plans were completed. Then it was suggested to CARE, an American organization which has done philanthropic work all over the world, particularly in Iran, that they might provide assistance for the project.

"A sum of $15,000 was given by CARE for the construction of the building and the purchase of the looms. Later CARE provided another $7,000 for raw materials. The transportation of the looms was handled through the Imperial Organization for Social Services. Engineer Sar Reshteh agreed to install the looms. Engineer Ashbeghi prepared the contracts for procurement of yarn and the marketing of finished fabrics through Mr. Siavashi who is the manager of Atlas Baf Factory."

For a moment memories of all the effort it had taken to accomplish that which could now be put in so few words swept through my mind and I was embarrassed to find my voice shaking with passion as I said:

"Let it not be hidden that this small project has taken six years to complete!"

Again I found myself speaking objectively, putting the memory of fruitless interviews, unanswered letters, drowned hopes, unexplainable disappointments, away from my mind.

"The object of the factory is not entirely financial profit though this is important if the factory is to be self-perpetuating. More important is that it will put to work the energies and talents of the people. It will be educational: the people of the village and their children will learn a profitable trade.

"The factory will be managed by an acting manager, a board of directors, all from the village of Sarbandan and under the direction of the cooperative.

"I wish to thank everyone who has helped me on this long and difficult road. I would particularly like to thank with sincerity the people of America, who through their contributions to CARE made this project possible. And my sincere thanks to Dr. Kline, who clothed the body of my dream in the coat of action—who helped to change a vision into reality.

"Thank you; thank you all."

A little after three the guests from Teheran left and the factory stockholders came into my home to eat the food that waited for them on the table. Mash'hadi Mokhtar, for the first time in many weeks, smiled, his gold teeth flashing under his magnificent mustache, and said, "This has been a great day for Sarbandan. A great day for all of us."

There was food left for the children who gathered outside, and my girls, with shining faces, moved among the people they had learned to love.

Later, much later, Shapoor and I sat on the steps of our house. The low-hanging sun made the wheat stubble in the field cast broken shadows and the field looked soft-patterned, like a carpet. Shapoor put his arm across my shoulder. "You are happy, Najmeh?"

"So happy, Shapoor."

"Are you satisfied now?"

I put my cheek against his shoulder. "Shapoor, I am never satisfied, never content. That is my problem. I see other things for Sarbandan, other advances for all of Iran."

"Poor Najmeh. Poor Najmeh-jun," he said, but there was no mockery in his voice.

We were silent until the sun disappeared and we sat in the gray of twilight.

"Najmeh, I have something to tell you." His voice was very low and I strained to hear every word. "I have been invited to go to Mecca. The invitation is from the Ministry of Foreign Affairs. I would like you to go, too."

"To Mecca?" Never had I thought seriously of going to Mecca. To Meshed, perhaps, to Ghom, to Najaf, but not to Mecca.

"We would not be together there, of course," he went on. "The ceremony separates the men and the women. But we would both have time to meditate, to pray, to know ourselves."

"Mecca," I said again. I remembered what I had heard of the hegira; of the people from every nation, black, brown, yellow, white, with many tongues but with one faith. I thought of the ceremonies that honored Abraham, Moses, Jesus, as well as Mohammed. I thought of the peace that can come to even troubled people in the presence of God, and I said something which made him look at me with brows drawn together in puzzlement. "I will go. There I can consecrate myself to becoming three willow trees making one shade."

"You speak in riddles, Najmeh," he said, and his arm tightened around my shoulder as we sat together in the silent dark.

If You Are Puzzled: A Glossary

aftabe: A narrow-necked jug or jar with a lip on one side, a handle on the other, used to carry water for personal cleansing.

Ali: A mysterious "animal" that the nomads of Dashte Moghan thought attended women at the time of delivery unless specific efforts were made to keep him out.

bapouk: An incurable disease prevalent in Sistan Baluchistan caused by drinking contaminated water.

bazaar: A complex of small shops and markets, many of them open and displaying goods on the ground along the narrow and sometimes dark corridors. Behind these shops that are open to all customers there is an inner bazaar where large deals are consummated. Sometimes such a term as "trade is in the bazaar stage" is used to describe the relationship between the merchant, his goods and his customer.

Bongha: An organization that is similar to a bureau in that it is part of the government, but more like a foundation in that it has the power to disperse funds. Under the father of the present Shah, urban and industrial development was stressed. Now the Development Bongha that endeavors to raise the standard of living in rural areas is gaining in importance.

CARE: An American organization known by its trademark, the CARE package. However, in areas like Iran CARE's work providing "self help" opportunities is even more important. It is not a self-perpetuating organization and leaves an area as soon as the local government can take over the projects.

chopogh: A kind of pipe for smoking tobacco, frequently used in a ceremonial manner.

Co-operatives: When the Iranian government undertook to divide large

209

land holdings among the individual farmers it met with many difficulties. These excellent farmers knew nothing about purchasing seed, insecticide, etc. They had experience with marketing. They had no money to buy equipment, sink wells, etc. Co-operatives were formed to give the farmers instruction and aid. In order to borrow money and take advantage of the other opportunities afforded co-operatives, the co-operative must be correctly registered with the government.

dashte: A plain. Dashte Moghan, the Plains of Moghan.

dehyar: A village worker, either man or woman. This individual is more than a social worker since he is expected to assume leadership in every phase of the village life.

garmsir: Winter-grazing land.

gendarme: More than a policeman, the gendarme is the arm of the government in rural villages and is expected to not only insure the safety of the people and maintain village peace and order, but has been expected to take charge of such chores as tax collection.

Ghom: A religious center closer to Teheran than any other. Non-Moslem visitors are not allowed in the great mosque.

Hafiz: One of Iran's greatest poets. Many of the concepts he presented have become folk wisdom.

haji: A hegira (pilgrimage) to a holy shrine; Mecca is the most important of these. All good Moslems hope to some day go on a haji to Mecca, though Mashed is also popular.

hammami: The bathkeeper.

hubbly-bubbly: A long pipe, sometimes with its bowl resting on the floor in which water is constantly boiling.

Isfahan: The capital city of Shah Abbas who ruled at the time of Elizabeth II. Isfahan is sometimes called "half the world." Its center square surrounded by mosques of incredible beauty and by the gateway to the bazaar, merits that title.

Italconsult: One of the great engineering consultation firms based in Rome, Italy. Iran has sought its exceptional engineering services.

ja-jim: a blanket, usually handwoven, not unlike the blankets of the Indians of the American Southwest.

jube: a stream of water that runs through the village furnishing the people with water for every purpose.

jun: Suffix meaning "dear." Often added to a name so frequently it becomes part of it. Najmeh-jun.

kadkhoda: The nearest English translation is mayor but that is not an exact definition. In the days of the absentee landlord the kadkhoda was his representative in the village, not only conducting its affairs but protecting the landlord's interests. In villages where the land is owned by the people the kadkhoda's position is more political, but he is not subject to democratic election.

karvanseras: At one time these were inns built on camel caravan routes.

khan: The head of a tribe, usually an hereditary position.

khorsee: A small fire of charcoal or dung is built under a sort of stool. A blanket covers the stool and touches the floor at every side. The heat from even a small fire concentrated under the blanket makes a warm place in the home.

koocheck: Little one.

korish: An excellent Persian food of lamb and vegetables.

Madar-i-Kadkhoda: Mother of the kadkhoda. This title is used instead of a name if one is fortunate enough to have such a son.

Meghs: Wise men; magi.

Mash'hadi: This title joined to a name means the bearer has been on a haji to Mashed.

mosque: A Moslem place of worship. The mosques in Iran, unlike those in Turkey, are usually open courts enclosed by walls which may be exquisite colonnades, may be made up of a series of open cublelui in which religious novitiates are studying or meditating, or may be simple walls. Large mosques have incredibly beautiful domes and minarets or prayer towers. Every mosque must have water available for the cleansing of the supplicant before prayer, and a niche which indicates the position of Mecca.

mullah: There is no priesthood, as such, in the Moslem religion. The mullah is especially educated to conduct such rituals as marriage, read the Koran from the minaret during Ramadan and make the call to prayer. Historically the mullah have been a power in politics.

Nassim: A zephyr, a soft breeze.

No Ruz: New Year's, which occurs on the exact beginning of the vernal equinox.

Persepolis: Perhaps the most remarkable ruins in the world; one of the capitals of the Medo-Persian Empire.

PLAN: An Iranian official government organization that studies the needs of the country, makes recommendations for the spending of money, and checks on the value received from money so spent.

Ramazan (also Ramadan): The month in which the Koran was revealed. It is now a time for fasting during the daylight hours.

reshteh-b-reshteh: A sweet cookie made from rice.

rish-e-safed: A village council. Strictly speaking, a council of elders.

sabseh: A plate of grain germinating in water. As the green shoots grow they absorb all of the unhappiness of the household.

Sahib: An Indian title for a man of position, also used in Baluchistan.

salaam: Persian greeting.

samovar: A tall container of brass, or silver, very beautiful, in which a flame keeps water boiling for tea. The *samovar* is in every home, no matter how humble that home is.

Sardar: The title of the khan in Baluchistan.

Saudi: A famous Persian poet.

Shahsavan: When Shah Abbas came to power he found that all of the fighting men were responsible to tribal khans. He formed an army of his own from seven tribes which, in true Persian style, became a separate tribe.

Shi'at Islam: The accepted faith of the Iranian Moslems. Islam was an Arabic religion and when the Arabs conquered Persia the Persians resisted the religion as well as the army. When they did accept the faith they continued to resist the leadership of Omar who had ordered the invasion of Iran and accepted, instead, Mohammed's son-in-law, Ali. When Ali became caliph (head of the Moslems) he was assassinated; his son Hassan was assassinated and finally when a younger son Hussein became caliph he was assassinated. The Shi'at part of Islam mourns the death of these martyrs. There are few differences in doctrine between the Shi'at and Sunni Moslems. They both pray in Arabic and follow the words of the Koran.

Shiraz: A beautiful city where the tombs of Hafiz and Saudi are popular shrines.

Sizdah-Bedar: Thirteenth day out. A day when everyone in Iran must go out for a picnic.

taushak: Bun made of bread dough with sugar and perhaps nuts added.

toutean: A very small fishing boat used for lake fishing.

ABOUT THE AUTHORS

NAJMEH NAJAFI was born in Teheran, the eighth child of a father who had been tutor and adviser to the last of the Kajar kings. A young woman of independent spirit, she studied dress design and, at the age of eighteen, opened her own shop in Teheran for a fashionable clientele.

But this was not what she wanted. In less than two years she closed her shop and came to the United States to study. While attending Pasadena City College she met Helen Hinckley (Mrs. Ivan Jones), who writes: "When Najmeh Najafi was a student she lived as a 'borrowed daughter' in our home. I became interested in Najmeh and her dream, and because her English was limited, I helped her to write her first book, *Persia Is My Heart,* which was published by Harper's in 1953.

"After she had been successful in Sarbandan we wrote *Reveille for a Persian Village,* which was published by Harper's in 1958. There, Najmeh met and married Shapoor Mozaffari, a technical expert with the Near East Foundation. They now have two children.

"In 1963, I, with my family, spent several weeks in Iran. At this time we were Najmeh's house guests. I found Iran to be exactly as I had pictured it and in many ways visiting there was like going home. After our return Najmeh visited in America again and had an idea for another book that would stress her work on the borders—the eastern border where she worked at Bampoor and the northern border where her work was centered at Alirezabad. We began to work on *A Wall and Three Willows.* It differs from the other two books in that Najmeh has matured, her outlook has been changed somewhat by this maturing, and the dreams that were only dreams in the first two books are fulfilled."

In addition to her own writing Helen Hinckley has taught a course in Writing for Publication at Pasadena City College for twenty years.

309.23

N16

55880